**COPTIC ORTHODOX
PATRIARCHATE**

See of St. Mark

LIFE OF FAITH

***BY
H. H. POPE SHENOUDA III***

Reprinted 2016 by St Shenouda Monastery Australia
by kind permission of H.H Pope Tawadros II

Title : Life of Faith
Author : H. H. Pope Shenouda Ill.
Press : Tebaa El Kawmia.
Edition : August 1989 - First edition.
Legal Deposit No.: 5606/1989
Revised : COEPA 1997

H.H. Pope Shenouda III, 117th Pope of Alexandria and the See of St. Mark

CONTENTS

In the name of the Father and of the Son and of the Holy Spirit One God. Amen.

INTRODUCTION

Faith is not merely adopting a set of beliefs that you may say in the "Creed", but a way of life or adherence to that which leads to life.

To what benefit is believing in God without having a relationship with him, obeying and loving Him?

In addition, what is the benefit of believing in eternity and in life after death if one does not prepare for it by repentance, spiritual vigil, and loving God?

And to what benefit is believing in virtues if one does not live them? Therefore there is a big difference between theoretical faith which does not save the soul, and practical faith, the fruits of which are evident in one's life.

This book was written to explain to you the meaning of faith, its stages and types and its importance in our lives and its greatness.

St. Paul wrote, *"Examine yourselves as to whether you are in the faith. Test yourselves. Do you not know yourselves"* (2 Cor. 13:5).

Not everyone who says he believes has faith, but is measured according to God's saying "You will know them by their fruits" (Matt. 7:16).

There are those who claim to have faith, but have neither the heart nor the life of a believer. So what then is the life of a believer?

The life of faith is linked with peace, tranquillity and lack of fear, for when you become afraid, then the Lord will say to you *"O you of little faith, why did you doubt?"* (Matt. 14:31).

The life of a believer is also associated with purity of behaviour, for the believer feels the presence of God, who sees, hears and records all that he does. For this reason the believer feels ashamed and afraid of wrong doing in front of God.

The life of a believer is a life of submission to the will of God. Having faith that God is the maker of all things, and all that He permits to happen is for our own good. In this way, God's children live in peace, happiness and satisfaction with all that God grants them.

The life of faith does not believe anything is impossible for the Lord, who said, *"All things are possible to him who believes"* (Mark 9:23).

Therefore the believer does not quiver in times of distress, but believes wholeheartedly that God has many solutions, and will interfere to fulfil His will.

The believer does not enter into an argument with God about His doing, but accepts all things and confidence in God's wisdom and love.

The believer concentrates on the unseen than the visible things, *"For the things which are seen are temporary, but the things which are not seen are eternal"* (2 Cor. 4:18).

The heroes of faith are not only those who defended their faith, but also those who lived a fruitful life of faith that worked in love.

This book before you, gives you a clarified ideas on the life of faith, how it acquired, and how to test if you are really in faith or not.

Pope Shenouda III

CHAPTER 1

HOW GREAT IS FAITH

The importance of faith is clearly seen in the apostle's words about the Lord, *"But without faith it is impossible to please Him"* (Heb. 11:6).

The importance of faith also shows in the apostle's description as one of the three great virtues *"faith, hope and love"* (1 Cor. 13:13) and the life of righteousness *"Now the just shall live by faith"* (Heb. 10:38).

Faith is the beginning of the road which leads to God, for how can you be united with God and God in you, to walk with Him and keep His commandments, if first, you do not believe in His existence, His divinity or in His book the Bible and all that it contains?

Thus, faith is the beginning of the road to God and an elementary necessity for salvation according to the Lord Himself *"He who believes and is baptised will be saved"* (Mark 16:16). *"That whoever believes in Him should not perish but have everlasting life"* (John 3:16). *"He who believes in Him is not condemned; but he who does not believe is condemned already"* (John 3:18). He also reprimanded the Jews by saying, *"You will die in your sins; for if you do not believe that I am He"* (John 8:24).

Salvation is available to every one through the blood of our Lord Jesus, but it can not save without faith. As St. Paul and Silas said to the Jail keeper "*Believe on the Lord Jesus Christ, and you will be saved, you and your household*" (Acts 16:31).

Through this faith, the gospels were written and preached by the apostles.

John, the evangelist inspired by the Holy Spirit, wrote "*But these are written that you may believe that Jesus is the Christ, the Son of God, and that believing you may have life in His name*" (John 20:31).

Faith is the beginning of a life with God. Faith is also our companion throughout our lives, and the importance of faith in its relationship with righteousness.

Thus spoke the apostle about righteousness that was credited to faith "*By his faith he condemned the world and became heir of the righteousness that comes by faith*" (Heb. 11:7). And about faith that was credited to righteousness, "*And it was credited to him as righteousness*" (James 2:23). The Bible also speaks of justification by faith, "*Therefore, having been justified by faith, we have peace with God through our Lord Jesus Christ*" (Rom.5:1).

Faith is a necessity to miracles and their acceptance. How great is our Lord's saying to the blind man of Jericho when He said, "*Your faith has healed you*" (Luke 18:42, Mark 10:52). And His saying to the man with leprosy, "*Your faith has made you well*" (Luke 17:19). To the sick woman He said, "*Take heart daughter, your faith has healed you*" (Matt. 9:22). When He heard the two blind men shouting *"Have mercy on us, Son of David"* (Matt. 9:29), He said to them, *"According to your faith will it be done to you"* and their sight was restored.

On the other hand, we see the Lord in His home town that *"He did not do many miracles there because of their lack of faith"* (Matt. 13:58).

The power of God can do miracles for you, but it awaits your faith. He will grant you according to your faith. For this reason, miracles happen to some and not to others although the power of God is the same.

What about he, who is weak in faith? He has to pray as did the boy's father who said, *"Lord, I believe; help my unbelief!"* (Mark 9:24). Here we see that God performs miracles in general according to faith, but on other occasions, He performs miracle that we may believe. In both cases faith is coupled with the miracle, either it comes before or is caused of it.

Faith, regardless of type, is a source of power.

It is sufficient that a person believes in an idea, so you see him working with Christ's power to carry it through. Faith gives him perseverance, might and courage which he would not have otherwise.

Thus, where there is faith there is power. A prayer in faith is a strong prayer. He who believes in prayer and its effect prays with warmth, assurance and power. A sermon preached by a person who believes in every word, makes a strong sermon, and through it, his faith is transmitted to the hearts of his listeners.

The importance of faith lies in its association with many virtues. The fruits of faith are strength, peace, courage, tranquillity and restfulness. Its fruits are a life of purity and righteousness, a life of submission and devotion to God, a life of prayer and many other virtues.

A few questions then come into mind:

-What is faith?
-What is faith, the basis of salvation and redemption?
-What is faith, the basis of all these virtues?
-What is faith, the basis of miracles and God's words who said, *"Everything is possible for him who believes"* (Mark 9:23)?

CHAPTER 2

WHAT IS FAITH?

Any worshipper of God can use the word 'faith' if when he does not believe in the Truth. He may have the name of a believer, but does not have the heart of one.

Faith does not automatically make you a believer if you are born a family which believes in the existence of God. But faith has a much deeper than this, it encompasses the whole spiritual life, performs miracles.

At one occasion, the disciples of the Lord were unable to heal a epileptic boy from the demon, so they asked the Lord for the reason and He answered them "Because of your unbelief" (Matt. 17:20) and rebuked them by saying "*O faithless and perverse generation*" (Matt 17:17).

A generation be unbelievers, which God came for, but where they really unbelievers? How alarming! Here the Lord says to His disciples "*I say to you, if you have faith as a mustard seed, you will say to this mountain, `Move from here to there,' and it will move*" (Matt. 17:20). Truly, what is this faith of a seed which can move a mountain? As the apostle says "*Examine yourselves as to whether you are in the faith. Test yourselves*" (2 Cor. 13:5).

The Bible tells us of something strange, more dangerous... what is it? It is the state of a human being who seems to be believing in God, he prays and performs miracles but he does not believe in Truth! and even not accepted in the eyes of God! Here is what the Lord Himself said "*Not everyone who says to Me, `Lord, Lord,' shall enter the kingdom of heaven*" (Matt 7:21). The Lord continues "Many will say to Me in that day, `Lord, Lord, have we not prophesied in Your name, cast out demons in Your name, and done many wonders in Your name?' And then I will declare to them, `I never knew you; depart from Me, you who practice lawlessness!' (Matt.7:22-23).

What shall we call those who say 'Lord, Lord... in your name we did this and that'? Are they really believers? Maybe it's only an apparent faith, or faith by name, or only mental faith, but it's not the real faith accepted by God.

What then is the real faith which is accepted in the eyes of the Lord? We ask Him and He answers "*Not everyone who says to Me, `Lord, Lord,' ... but he who does the will of My Father in heaven* " (Matt. 7:21). This also reminds us of the story of the five virgins who also used the expression 'Lord, Lord,...' and they stood behind the closed door saying "*Lord, Lord open the door for us", and they heard from the Lord the clear and terrifying answer "I tell you the truth, I don't know you"*.

The expression 'Lord, Lord' does not necessarily help if you are awaiting the bridegroom with a lamp without oil, or if you arrive after the door is closed.

Therefore what is faith? and what is its connection to oil which signifies the Holy Spirit? and what is its connection with the will of God who is in heaven?

This faith is alive and is accepted by God as we'll see later... Faith is not simply a belief but also a life.

You can test it by its fruits in your life... as the Lord said "*You will know them by their fruits....every good tree bears good fruit, but a bad tree bears bad fruit. Therefore by their fruits you will know them"* (Matt. 7:16-20).

This is how you can test yourself: Does your faith bear fruit? Because 'by their fruits you will recognise them'.

This is what John the evangelist teaches us "*Now by this we know that we know Him"* how? *"If we keep His commandments. He who says, "I know Him," and does not keep His commandments, is a liar, and the truth is not in him* " (1 John 2:3-4). Faith is tested through a life of obedience to God's commandments, and he who does not have this obedience is not considered a believer of Truth, and can not claim to know God.

The apostle Paul lists in his letter to the Hebrews (Heb. 11) wonderful examples of faithful men. They show practical faith in their private lives. Enoch for example; the bible did not say that he defended his belief like other heroes of faith. But Enoch was a hero of faith because he "*He pleased God.*" (Heb. 11:5) and "Walked with God" (Gen. 5:22,24).

You may not be as spiritually knowledgeable as were the apostles, but no doubt you can also lead the same life as our father Enoch, who walked with God. You can live like other men of faith who St. Paul mentioned "*They were strangers and pilgrims on the earth... they desire a better, that is, a heavenly country.*" (Heb 11: 13,16).

Our father Abraham was a man of faith who "*Obeyed when he was called to go out* " (Heb. 11: 8), and went out after God "*Not knowing where he was going.*" He was a man of faith in accepting God's timing and even when he was to sacrifice his only son, confident that God can raise the dead (Heb. 11:17-19).

His wife Sarah is also considered a hero of faith because she believed the Lord for *"She judged Him faithful who had promised."* (Heb 11:11).

Heroes of faith are not only those who defended their belief, but are also those who believed in the Lord, walked with Him, who were righteous and pleased Him (Heb. 11:33). Also those who "*Were tortured, not accepting deliverance, that they might obtain a better resurrection.*" and those who "*Had trial of mockings and scourgings, yes, and of chains and imprisonment. .. of whom the world was not worthy* " (Heb. 11:35-38) *"And all these, having obtained a good testimony through faith"* (Heb. 11:39). In all these examples, the bible gives us a wide spectrum of the meaning of faith.

Paul tells us that faith "*Is the substance of things hoped for, the evidence of things not seen*" (Heb. 11:1).

You hope for many things after death. You hope for eternal life with angels and the saints, to see the Lord in Paradise and resurrect from the dead into a spiritual body. You desire eternal peace after the general resurrection. Faith is without any doubt, complete confidence that these matters exist without having seen them.

Faith Is Beyond The Level Of Our Senses

Faith does not contradict but beyond our senses. Faith is a higher power than our limited senses. Our senses are only capable of detecting physical or materialistic things, but there are other matters, which are beyond the material sense. The senses are also limited in what they can physically detect.

Instruments are often used to sense details and gain information which the senses alone can not accomplish. How much more is it for the non-physical, which the apostle called "invisible things". Faith is not what is seen by the human eye (2 Cor. 5:7). The soul can not be seen or felt by the senses. The fact that the senses do not feel the soul does not mean that it does not exist but rather, unable to detect it. The senses are limited in scope and the level of the soul.

Faith Is Beyond The Level Of The Intellect

The intellect may guide you to the beginning of the way but faith continues with you on the way to the end. Faith does not contradict the intellect, but leads it to a higher level the mind alone cannot reach.

What the mind cannot understand is called unattainable. We often describe God as infinite because He has no limit. The human mind is limited, and can only understand the limited matters. The mind can bring you to know God and some of His qualities but of faith, "*God has revealed... to us through His Spirit.*" (1 Cor. 2:10). God shows Himself to the believer to what they can bear to comprehend.

The mind may not grasp many things but must accept them. By nature, the mind does not refuse all that it does not understand. There are for example in our physical world, many inventions only experts can understand. In spite of this, the normal mind can accept and deal with these things without knowing how they work. The mind accepts death, and speaks about it, but does not understand it.

If the mind accepts many things in our world without understanding them, then clearly nothing should deprive the mind from accepting other matters not of this world.

The mind does not understand how miracles happen, but it accepts them and finds joy in them.

A miracle is called a miracle because the mind fails to grasp it and cannot explain it. But the mind accepts it by faith... faith, with infinite power, greater than that of the mind, can perform things the mind fails to understand. This power is the power of God the almighty.

We respect the mind, and at the same time we know its limits. We can not accept the proud mind which desires to understand all things, refusing that some are beyond comprehension.

The mind should be humble to know its limitation *"For I say, through the grace given to me, to everyone who is among you, not to think of himself more highly than he ought to think, but to think soberly, as God has dealt to each one a measure of faith"* (Rom. 12.3). The mind should submit matters beyond its level of understanding to faith.

If the mind wanted to nullify all that it does not understand it would end up destroying itself, lose the element of faith and put itself in a very narrow circle of very limited range of understanding.

Believers are moderate, they esteem the mind and use it in religious and spiritual affairs. There are philosophers and people of high intellect among the believers, who do not depend on the mind in pride or trust in its ability to understand all things. However, in simplicity and humility they confess that their minds are limited and are unable to understand all this associated with God. With faith, their hearts and minds accept all that is beyond the level of the mind.

The simple and humble mind accepts faith and miracles.

We mean humble in the sense that the mind is not proud of its own understanding or destroys all that is does not understand. But does not complicate matters or insist on placing everything within its own limits. We will refer to this point later when we speak about the simplicity of faith.

Faith is not only a prayer said, but a life we live. If you are living a life of faith, the fruits of faith apparent in your practical life. Examine your faith against the virtues which are clear in the believer's life and these are many. As the apostle says, *"Examine yourselves as to whether you are in the faith"* (2 Cor. 13:5).

Conviction Of The Unseen

The apostle said about faith: "*Faith is the substance of things hoped for, the evidence of things not seen*" (Heb. 11:1). We want to know what this verse means:

Conviction: is certainty, confidence and belief without doubt. It is not simply an idea, opinion or knowledge gained from reading or hearing about it, but certainty that unseen matters exist.

Here is a clear difference between believers and men of science. The things that are not seen are not in the working field of the researchers. If they are not sure of something, they investigate it thoroughly with their instruments and apparatus. The same also applies to men of material beliefs.

Believers are not like this, they follow God's saying "*Blessed are those who have not seen and yet have believed*" (John 20:29).

The believer accepts the creation from nothing. The scientist's research refuses this matter, and refuses that five loaves of bread fed five thousand men (excluding the women and children) and that twelve baskets full of bread where left over. The believer accepts all this.

The believer accepts firstly that God is powerful. He also accepts everything in a certain range of this unlimited power.

The believer frees himself from the doubts of the researches and the investigations of the unbeliever. Not only does he accept the unseen, but moreover, he lives according to and focuses his mind and affection on the unseen according to what the apostle's words. "*While we do not look at the things which are seen, but at the things which are not seen. For the things which are seen are temporary, but the things which are not seen are eternal.*" (2 Cor. 4:18).

You will ask, how can I see the hidden? And I tell you by faith. What are then those unseen matters? The first is probably God Himself, His qualities, His works, and all things pertaining to Him.

1- God, His Qualities And Works

God is unseen, as John the evangelist said "*No one has seen God*" (John 1:18). Actually who can see the divinity? No one! However, in spite of this, you believe in Him with all your heart, and with all certainty. This faith does not at all rely on your physical senses. You may say you see Him with your trained spiritual senses (Heb.5:14). This non-physical senses were trained to see the unseen, and we have the following examples from the Bible:

David said "*I have set the Lord always before me; Because He is at my right hand I shall not be moved.*" (Ps 16:8). So how did he see the Lord in front of him and at his right hand all times? No doubt he saw Him with an eye of faith. In some of the translations it is written "*I have seen the Lord....*" that means that he is continuously seeing the unseen and focusing on Him with mind and feeling.

With the same meaning Elijah said "*As the Lord of hosts lives, before whom I stand*"(1 Kin 18:15). How was he able to feel that he stands before God? And how was he able to always see the Lord in front of him? Not through the bodily senses since they can not arouse a believer's heart. But it is by faith that the Lord is before him. It is faith that sees the unseen.

If you are in faith, you will have confidence that God is always before you and will act according to this belief, that God sees you and hears you...

If you live in faith, you are sure that God is in the midst of His people, according to His promise "*...I am there in the midst of them*" (Matt. 18:20) and "*I am with you always, even to the end of the age.*" (Matt.28:20). You do not see Him with the eye of your body, but you believe that He is in our midst. You do not need to see Him physically to believe. You believe without seeing, or you perceive the unseen.

What is a spiritual life my brothers and sisters? It is not simply a shift from what is felt and visible to the unseen.

We live the unseen with confidence that He is in front of us. This becomes the difference between the believer and the non-believer.

The non-believer desires to see everything with his eyes, or else he can not believe. The believer does not allow his eyes, senses, or external happenings shape his beliefs. But his heart believes in the existence of unseen matters. On one occasion, God rebuked His disciple Thomas who would not believe without seeing when God said to him "*Do not be unbelieving, but believing*", "*Because you have seen Me, you have believed. Blessed are those who have not seen and yet have believed*" (John 20:27,29).

We mentioned earlier, faith in God is among the conviction of unseen matters. Not only faith in the existence of God but also faith in His attributes and in His works.

You believe in His goodness and choices for your good, the almighty who has dominion over all things. You believe that He is able to do everything, for "*The things which are impossible with men are possible with God*" (Luke 18:27), and you believe in God's love for you and for others.

You may not see all these qualities physically, but you believe in them. You believe that God takes care of the universe, and preserves its beauty. You believe that He labours and takes care of every individual. You will either see His work or the results of His work or you will not see anything at all.

2- The Timing Of God

The following were described as men of faith "*These all died in faith, not having received the promises, but having seen them afar off were assured of them, embraced them and confessed that they were strangers and pilgrims on the earth.* " (Heb. 11:13), these people waited for the things promised in faith, and believed in what the Lord said to them.

And things promised "*Which God has prepared for those who love Him*" were all unseen matters, as explained by the apostle as "*Eye has not seen, nor ear heard, Nor have entered into the heart of man*" (1 Cor. 2:9).

God's warnings are also unseen things. Noah believed the Lord when He said that He will flood the whole world even though floods were unknown to Noah. No flood had ever happened before in his days or the days of his ancestors. However, he believed that this which never happened before, would happen. He laboured to complete the ark, enduring the mockery from others, these were years of faith.

Noah heeded to the warning of God, and was therefore considered a man of faith. Through faith he had seen the flood before it happened. Through faith, he entered the ark with his wife, his sons and his son's wives. Our teacher Saint Paul teaches us, "*By faith Noah, being divinely warned of things not yet seen, moved with godly fear, prepared an ark for the saving of his household* " (Heb. 11:7). The others, who did not heed God's warning, and had no faith in God's truth were destroyed.

Lot and the city of Sidom also experienced God's warning before it happened. As this was the first time that fire came down from heaven, it was also the first time that a flood happened in the time of Noah.

The people of Sidom who did not accept the warning of God were destroyed as were who also did not believe it in the days of Noah.

God's warning in regard to eternity and judgement lies ever before us. Inspite of this, many are still immersed in evil and sin as if God had not warned them. They do not fear God in their hearts or judgement in eternity.

We spoke about God, His attributes and works, His promises and warmings as unseen matters, we should also add that:

3- Dwelling Of The Spirit And His Work In Us Are Unseen Matters

Samuel anointed David with oil and the spirit of the Lord came upon him (2 Sam. 16:13). No one saw the unseen Spirit of the lord, but it happened.

No one was able to see the Holy Spirit descend on the new believers when the disciples place their hands on them (Acts 8:17). The Holy Spirit also came on those anointed (1 John 2:20,27). No one saw the Holy Spirit but its fruits showed in their life.

You may be aware that there is an inner power working in you and for you, without your seeing it. It is what the Lord said "*But you shall receive power when the Holy Spirit has come upon you*" (Acts 1:8). This power, the power of the Holy Spirit, guides you to do good, helps you and protects you from sin.

Here we say that our whole life becomes in fellowship with the Holy Spirit (2 Cor. 13:14).

What is this fellowship? How does it take place? How can we be in fellowship with the Godly nature, this an unseen nature? We believe in God's active spirit working in the church, we do not see it but we believe in it.

The apostle said, "*Do you not know that you are the temple of God and that the Spirit of God dwells in you?*"(1 Cor.3:16), "*Do you not know that your body is the temple of the Holy Spirit who is in you, whom you have from God?*" (1 Cor. 6:19).

We do not see the Spirit, but we see its fruits.

The Lord said that through the fruits of the holy spirit, we can stand before governors and kings, "*For it is not you who speak, but the Spirit of your Father who speaks in you*" (Matt. 10:20). How does the Spirit of the Father Spirit speak through us? All these things are unseen matters.

4- The Grace Of God In Us Are Things Unseen.

We attain visits of grace, which fill us with God's love. We do not see it but we feel it. Grace working in us, is without doubt is the work of the unseen things.

Saint John the evangelist said "*Grace and truth came through Jesus.*" (John 1: 17). What is this grace working in us? And the grace that Saint John enjoyed. He said "*But by the grace of God I am what I am, and His grace toward me was not in vain.*" (1

Cor. 15: 10), and he also says about us "*For sin shall not have dominion over you, for you are not under law but under grace.*" (Rom. 6:14), and urges Timothy to "*Be strong in the grace that is in Christ Jesus.*" (2 Tim. 2: 1).

We do not see this grace with our physical eye, it is amongst the unseen matters, but we feel its presence in our lives. The grace of God in us is beyond our senses as we accept this grace from God. The church grants grace every time it repeats Saint Paul's words "*The grace of the Lord Jesus Christ, and the love of God, and the communion of the Holy Spirit be with you all.*" (2 Cor. 13:14).

Here we move to another point, the element of blessings

5- Blessing Are Unseen

A blessing can be directly from God, from parents, from the church through the priest and all these are unseen matters.

God said to Abram father of fathers "*I will make you a great nation; I will bless you And make your name great; And you shall be a blessing. I will bless those who bless you ... And in you all the families of the earth shall be blessed*" (Gen. 12:2,3). Abram saw the fruits of this unseen blessings in his life. Isaac blessed his son Jacob and he became blessed. Esau lamented because he lost this blessing (Gen.27). Jacob blessed Ephraim and Manasseh by saying "*The Angel who has redeemed me from all evil, Bless the lads*" (Gen. 48:16). Ephraim became exceedingly blessed, more than his brother when Jacob placed his right hand on Ephraim's head (Gen. 48:17-20).

What is this blessing? How was it passed from the hands of Isaac and Jacob? How was it given through the apostles, and from the hands of the men of faith?

All these unseen matters we believe in and in its blessings although we do not see them. We ask for the blessings of our mothers, fathers, from priests and men of God. Abram was a blessing to the world according to the Lord's promise to him. Joseph was also a blessing in the house of his master and to all Egypt, as was the blessings of Elijah.

Through all the above examples, we would still be unable to give a precise meaning to the word blessings, for it has wider meaning than our limited vocabulary can describe. An unseen matter, which we can only see its fruits. However, a blessing itself, who can see it and define it?

How was Jesus Christ able to bless through His hands the five loaves of bread and the two fish? This food given out was enough to feed thousands of people, and despite this, twelve full baskets were left over? How did this happen? What was the cause and its effect?. All these things are unseen matters.

6-Faith In The Presence Of Angels And Their Works

We believe in the existence of angels, and the unseen spirits. We may not have seen an angel in our whole life, but despite of this, we believe they close to us "*The angel of the Lord encamps all around those who fear Him, And delivers them.* " (Ps 34:7). We believe that the angels fill the church, and have confidence that they are with us in all that we do "*Are they not all ministering spirits sent forth to minister for those who will inherit salvation?*" (Heb. 1:14).

Many are glad if they see the Virgin Mary or the saints in a revelation.

It is far greater to believe that they are around you without seeing them. It is not necessary that God sends you a white dove during your evening church meetings, but you believe without seeing that the church is full of the spirits of angels. And the wings of the saints flutter upon it, the saints that God sent to serve humanity.

Gehazi the disciple of Elisha was afraid when he saw the enemies surrounding the city, but Elisha, the man with opened eyes saw the angels defending the it against the enemy. He comforted his disciple by saying "*Do not fear, for those who are with us are more than those who are with them*" (2 Kin 6:16). Elisha prayed that God would open the eyes of Gehazi to see and the conviction in unseen matters.

7- Belief In The Spirit And The Other World

We can not see the spirit, but presume its existence. When a person dies, we say that his spirit, which we have not seen, has left his body.

Faith is concerned with the destiny of this spirit, if it will go to heaven or to hell. Likewise, with the return of this spirit to the body in the general resurrection, and the destiny of the resurrected person in eternity after the last judgment.

All these matters, the spirit, resurrection, eternity, judgment, heaven, grace, hell, are all unseen matters and through faith we have a conviction in those things. Actually, no one can speak about the eternal life, and all things associated with it, except by faith. Likewise, he who believes in the second life believes in unseen matters.

8- People Believed In The Coming Of Christ Without Seeing Him

Even the Samaritan woman said to the Lord "*I know that Messiah is coming" (who is called Christ). "When He comes, He will tell us all things*" (John 4:25).

Thus, everyone knew, according to God's promise that the Messiah was coming. They were eagerly awaiting for Him. They understood what had Isaiah said, "*Behold, the virgin shall conceive and bear a Son, and shall call His name Immanuel*" (Isaiah 7:14). They believed nevertheless, although they never saw the Virgin.

The wait by the Old Testament people through faith for the Messiah is like our wait for the Second Coming of Christ in the New Testament. Waiting for Christ's Second Coming on the clouds according to the Lord's promise (Mat. 24:25) and the two angels who appeared to the disciples (Acts 1: 11).

We probably have not seen the Lord on the clouds in the glory of His Father and His saints. And through faith, we believe in His Second Coming in this form although we have never seen it.

9-Redemption Is Also From The Unseen Matters

Jesus redeemed us by taking away all our sins and dying for us through His love "*All we like sheep have gone astray; We have turned, every one, to his own way; And the Lord has laid on Him the iniquity of us all.*" (Isaiah 53:6). John the Baptist also said about Him "*Behold! The Lamb of God who takes away the sin of the world!*" (John 1:29). John the evangelist said "*And He Himself is the propitiation for our sins, and not for ours only but also for the whole world.*" (1 John 2:2). St. Paul said "*Having wiped out the handwriting of requirements that was against us.*" (Col.2:14), and "*having made peace through the blood of His cross*" (Col. 1:20).

We only see the cross; some may see it superficially! But, all gifts the cross has from love, redemption, forgiveness, cancelling of the written code, taking away the sins of the world, and also what the cross carries from peace, all these are unseen matters. We see them through faith.

Peter - before believing in all this - saw the cross as loss and as shame! Therefore he said "*Never, Lord*" (John 16:22). The Lord rebuked him because Peter did not see the unseen matters...

The cross represents the goodness of God to us. The rulers at that time did not see this because their eyes were blinded, "*For had they known, they would not have crucified the Lord of glory.*" (1 Cor. 2:8).

10- The Hidden Benevolences Of God

We only thank God for the benevolences we see and know. However, there are also unseen things we should thank Him for. When we enter the life of faith we automatically enter in a life of perpetual appreciation, as the apostle said "*Giving thanks always for all things to God the Father in the name of our Lord Jesus Christ*" (Eph. 5:20).

In our life, we also have to thank for the temptations, because we feel that they have hidden benevolences in them from God that we do not see. And if we saw them we'll no doubt be singing with James "*Count it all joy when you fall into various trials*" (James 1:2).

From this, we see that faith gives a spiritual meaning to suffering, pains that God allows for the special grace that is in them. All from unseen matters, but we accept them in faith having confidence in God's love who does good. We also have confidence in what the Bible says "*We know that all things work together for good to those who love God.*" (Rom. 8:28).

11-The Existence Of God In Our Lives And His Power Working In Us.

How beautiful is the Lord's saying to Jacob "*I am with you and will keep you wherever you go, and will bring you back to this land.*" (Gen. 28: 15). The Lord was with him and watched over him wherever he went although he has not seen the Lord physically. It is very comfortable for the soul to feel that the Lord is with us and to believe it. This allows us to live in serenity and joy.

The above was not only a blessing to Jacob but the Lord says "*I am with you always, even to the end of the age.*" (Matt. 28:20).

Our feeling that God is with us, gives us a feeling that a Godly power is walking with us and protecting us.

This power is working in you and is with you from the moment you receive the Holy Spirit and He then accompanies you for the rest of your life. In the time of the first church the people saw the kingdom of God being established in power (Mark 9: 1), "*And they were all filled with the Holy Spirit, and they spoke the word of God with boldness.*" (Acts 4:31). It was said that St. Stephen was "*Full of faith and power, did great wonders and signs*" (Acts 6:8), and that he stood before the synagogue "*And they were not able to resist the wisdom and the Spirit by which he spoke*" (Acts 6: 10). That is the power in faith. He who believes but is afraid to show his faith is a person with weak faith, he does not believe in the power of God working with him.

The woman who was bleeding for twelve years felt that if she could just touched the edge of the cloak of Jesus a power would come out of Him to heal her, and that is what happened (Matt. 9:22, Lk 8:46).

If you believe in the power of God and hold steadfastly to it, you will surely obtain it.

Let it be that you have this faith and this feeling in all aspects of your life: in your service, prayer and works.

Even in your fall, believe that there is a power to save you. If you are weaker than the devils then believe that God who loves you is stronger, and that He is able to save you from sin. And in strong faith pray to God to grant you the power you need to succeed in your spiritual life, ask Him who "*always leads us in triumph in Christ*" (2 Cor. 2:14).

Even if you have been waiting long time, just believe that the power of God will reach you and save you. This power of God is unseen, but it exists, and is ready to work with those who ask for it by faith. You need to experience this power which is accompanying you, not only in the life of repentance but in all aspects of your spiritual life so that when you speek, others will feel the strength and the effect of the words you are saying.

The believer is a strong person believing in the power of God working in him.

Paul said, "*To this end I also labour, striving according to His working which works in me mightily.*" (Col. 1:29) and he says about God "*To Him who is able to do exceedingly abundantly above all that we ask or think, according to the power that works in us.*" (Eph. 3:20).

It is faith in the unseen power of God that prompted Saint Paul to claim confidently, "*I can do all things through Christ who strengthens me.*" (Phil. 4:13).

We ask ourselves: is this phrase only applies to Saints like Paul? The Lord answers "*If you can believe, all things are possible to him who believes.*" (Mark 9:23).

Perhaps this power is a test for our spiritual lives. Are we in faith? Is it a power we are glad of and live in serenity with?

In the church, we rejoice in the many unseen things.

12-What Happens In The Baptism

Saint Paul says "*For as many of you as were baptised into Christ have put on Christ.*" (Gal. 3:27). How great is this sacrament! Who has seen its promise? Ananias told Saul, "*And now why are you waiting? Arise and be baptised, and wash away your sins.*" (Acts 22:16). Who saw these sins being washed away? These are unseen matters, which we accept by faith, as the apostle about Christ, "*He saved us, through the washing of regeneration and renewing of the Holy Spirit*" (Tit. 3: 5). The salvation we obtain by rebirth is an unseen matter, but we believe in it according to the Lord's saying, "*He who believes and is baptised will be saved.*" (Mark 16:16).

What is the meaning of a second birth? Moreover, what does it mean to be born from above, from God, and to be born from water and spirit? The Lord spoke about it in (John 3:3-6). They are all unseen matters; the rebirth from God is an unseen sacrament. We see a person immersed in the baptism font but we do not see how he is reborn from the spirit. Blessed are those who believe without seeing. This, the church calls a sacrament.

The apostle says "*Buried with Him in baptism, in which you also were raised with Him through faith ... forgiven you all trespass*" (Col. 2:12). He gives the same meaning in his letter to the Romans, and he adds that the old person was crucified with Christ, that we may live with Him (Rom. 6:3-6). Who has seen this death, burial, resurrection, forgiveness of sins, the new life, crucifixion of the old self... these are all unseen matters, but we believe in them.

13-The Sacrament Of The Holy Eucharist

You see in faith the bread and wine in front of you transform into the body and the blood of the Lord. Here you can not rely on your senses to judge, because the bodily senses see only the visible matters. But the spiritual senses heed to what the Lord says "This is my body... This is my blood" (Matt. 26:26,28), "*Unless you eat the flesh of the Son of Man and drink His blood, you have no life in you... My flesh is food indeed, and My blood is drink indeed. He who eats My flesh and drinks My blood abides in Me, and I in him.*" (John 6:53-56).

I do not dispute what the Lord said but I accept it in faith.

In faith we are sure of what we do not see for what is seen is bread and wine. This is what Saint Paul says "*The cup of blessing which we bless, is it not the communion of the blood of*

Christ? The bread which we break, is it not the communion of the body of Christ?" (1 Cor. 10:16), and he also says "*Therefore whoever eats this bread or drinks this cup of the Lord in an unworthy manner will be guilty of the body and blood of the Lord. For he who eats and drinks in an unworthy manner eats and drinks judgment to himself, not discerning the Lord's body.*" (1 Cor. 11:27,29).

How can we know if this is the body of the Lord, so as not to gain judgment upon ourselves? Here, by faith, we go beyond the level of the senses, and the level of the intellect.

Our minds make us tired when we accept the sacraments of the church. Our senses do also tire us. We need the simplicity of faith to believe all what Jesus Christ and the apostles said without discussion.

14-To Accept The Sacraments Of Christianity

To accept the laying of hands that Barnabas and Saul obtained from the disciples, so that they could go on to service (Acts 13:2,3), and also the laying of Saint Paul's hands on Timothy (2 Tim. 1:6). We believe that this is a sacrament.

We accept the power the Lord gave in His saying "*If you forgive the sins of any, they are forgiven them; if you retain the sins of any, they are retained* " (John 20:23) "*Whatever you bind on earth will be bound in heaven, and whatever you loose on earth will be loosed in heaven.*" (Matt. 18:18).

This honour is unseen but we see it through faith. It is not for everyone and no one can take it by himself, but he who is called by God just like Aaron was (Heb. 5:4).

Seeing the unseen is the real spiritual sight: maybe it is what the Lord meant in His saying to his disciples "*But blessed are your eyes for they see* " (Matt. 13:16). What do they see? It sees Jesus Christ and His miracles. It sees the unseen just like the revelation, which Saint John saw. Further, how Saint Paul saw the third heaven and many other signs (2 Cor.12: 2,7).

The Lord rebuked those who did not have this spiritual sense by saying "*And their eyes they have closed, Lest they should see with their eyes* " (Matt. 13: 15) the disciple also wrote the same thing about them (Acts 28:27). The expression they closed their eyes could mean that they did not train themselves to see the spiritualities or that they refused to see the spiritualities because of their interest in material things.

Gehazi did not see what his teacher Elisha saw (2 Kin 6:17). The companions of Saul did not see anything during the Godly vision he saw, the Bible said that they "*Stood speechless, hearing a voice but seeing no one.*" (Acts 9:7).

CHAPTER 3

DEGREES AND KINDS OF FAITH

Degrees Of Faith

People differentiate from one another in the kind of faith and the degree of faith they have "*As God has dealt to each one a measure of faith*" (Rom. 12:3).

Some may exaggerate by saying that a person with little faith is not at all a believer. This judgment is against the teachings of the Holy Bible, as we will see later. Some may mix between the word 'believer' and 'the chosen one', as if these two words mean the same thing. Let us then meditate on the different kinds of faith and its degrees.

1. There is the newly converted believer and the apostle ordered not to swell the believer up with pride or else he will "*fall into the same condemnation as the devil.*" (1 Titus. 3:6).

2. There are those with little or weak faith, following are examples from Bible about this kind:

a) Those who complain about God's care in food or clothes. The Lord gave them an example of the lilies of the field, and that not even Solomon in all his splendour was dressed like one of these. The Lord then rebuked them by saying "*Now if God so clothes the grass of the field, which today is, and tomorrow is thrown into the oven, will He not much more clothe you, O you of little faith?*" (Matt. 6:28-30, Luke 12:28).

b) The Lord also rebuked the disciples, when they thought that they did not take bread with them by saying "*O you of little faith*" (Matt. 14:31).

c) The Lord rebuked Saint Peter when he became afraid after walking with Him on the water and began to sink, the Lord rebuked him and said "*O you of little faith, why did you doubt*" (Matt. 14:31).

d) Similarly, when the disciples got frightened when the waves covered the ship during the Lord's sleep, then the Lord said to them "*Why are you fearful, O you of little faith?*" (Matt. 8:26).

Thus fear and doubt in the help of the Lord are evidences of little faith.

e) The apostle gave an example of a person of weak faith who eats only vegetables, the apostle also ordered that one should not judge or mock such a person and said "*To his own master he stands or falls. Indeed, he will be made to stand, for God is able to make him stand.*" (Rom. 14:1-4).

Here I admire the father of the boy with an evil spirit, when the Lord asked him "*do you believe?*" so as to heal his son, the father answered "*Lord, I believe; help my unbelief!*" (Mark 9:24).

The person with weak faith needs those who pray for him, so that the Lord may help him. We should not mock him for God is able to make him firm in faith.

3. There Is A Third Kind Of Faith And That Is The Limited Faith

We mean by that the person who believes in the Lord but in certain limits, and his faith does not exceed these limits. An example of this kind of faith are Mary and Martha, who believed that the Lord is able to heal their brother from sickness so as not to die. If he dies however, then their faith was not yet that far that his being risen from the dead was possible.

Therefore, each one of them said to the Lord "*If You had been here, my brother would not have died.*" (John 11:21,32). When the Lord said to Martha "*your brother will rise again*" she answered Him "*I know that he will rise again in the resurrection at the last day* " (John 11:24) and when the Lord went to the tomb and said "*take away the stone*" Martha said "*Lord, by this time there is a stench, for he has been dead four days*" (John 11:39).

God did not refuse this limited faith but He gave it a chance to grow.

That's why He said to Martha "*He who believes in Me, though he may die, he shall live.*" and He rebuked her at the tomb by saying "*Did I not say to you that if you would believe you would see the glory of God?*" (John 11:25,40). He gave her the chance to see the glory of God in rising her brother Lazarus from the dead, so that she believes and also the Jews, who saw the miracle, would also believe.

Here faith came after the miracle and not before it.

May be it happened like that because this miracle was the first of its kind, namely rising a dead after four days of being dead and stinking.

4. A fourth kind, from the weak faith, **is the slow heart in faith**. Maybe it comes from a slow understanding, or from no comprehension, so the person's faith does not come quickly. This was the kind of faith the disciples of Emmaus had in respect to the resurrection of the Lord. The Lord rebuked them by saying "*O foolish ones, and slow of heart to believe in all that the prophets have spoken! Ought not the Christ to have suffered these things*" (Luke 24:25-26). He then began to explain to them what was written in all the Scriptures concerning Christ. so that they believed, or so that he cures this tardiness in their faith resulting from their little knowledge or little understanding.

In this example we could also say that it is sound to rectify the misunderstandings concerning the faith. It is much better that way than to despise and to mock such persons, it won't bring any good results and it won't read to the real faith.

5. There Is A Dangerous Case Of Faith And That Is The Dead Faith.

Saint James the apostle said, "*Faith by itself, if it does not have works, is dead.*" (James 2:17,20). He also said that this kind of faith can not save the person (James 2:14) and he saw that the living faith should have works or deeds to show it, "*I will show you my faith by my works.*" (James 2:18).

6. There Is Also Faith Which Is Not Firm

An example of that is Jesus Christ before being arrested, said to His disciple Peter "*Satan has asked for you, that he may sift you as wheat. But I have prayed for you, that your faith should not fail*" (Luke 22:31,32). At this time Peter's faith failed but he turned back again to his first power.

7. There Are Other Cases The Bible Describes As Deviating From The True Faith:

a) Saint Paul the apostle said "*But if anyone does not provide for his own, and especially for those of his household, he has denied the faith and is worse than an unbeliever.*" (1 Tim. 5:8).

b) He said about the young widows when their sensual desires overcame their dedication to Christ "*They desire to marry, having condemnation because they have cast off their first faith.*" (1 Tim. 5:11,12).

c) He also said *"For the love of money is a root of all kinds of evil, for which some have strayed from the faith in their greediness, and pierced themselves through with many sorrows* " (1 Tim. 6: 10).

d) He said "*Guard what was committed to your trust, avoiding the profane and idle babblings and contradictions of what is falsely called knowledge by professing it some have strayed concerning the faith"* (1 Tim. 6:20,21).

In all these examples, can we deny the relationship between faith and deeds?

With a false deed it is said that a person denied the faith, or refused it, or went astray from it, or deviated from it. May be with these examples as measures we can examine ourselves, doing what the apostle said: "*Examine yourselves as to whether you are in the faith.*" (2 Cor. 13: 5).

8. The Most Dangerous Case Is To Retreat From Faith

The apostle says "*In latter times some will depart from the faith, giving heed to deceiving spirits and doctrines of demons*" (1 Tim. 4: 1). The expression to retreat from faith means that they were in faith and then they retreated from it.

The apostle speaks about the great retreat that will happen before the coming of Christ "*for that day will not come until the rebellion occurs*" (2 Thes. 2:3).

This is from the general point of view but from the individual point of view the apostle says "*Now the just shall live by faith; But if anyone draws back, My soul has no pleasure in him*" (Heb. 10:38). Here he speaks about the retreat of a believer who was living in faith.

So long the believer can retreat so the believers are not the chosen ones, because the chosen ones stay in their faith all their lives until they meet the Lord.

The above are illustrations of negative kinds of faith, let us explain the positive ones.

9. To Grow In Faith

Saint Paul the apostle says to the Thessalonians "*We are bound to thank God always for you, brethren,... because your faith grows exceedingly*" (2 Thes. 1: 3) and he also said to the people of Corinth that their faith increases (2 Cor. 8:7).

Faith is a virtue like all the other virtues, one can grow in it.

10. To Keep The Faith And To Maintain It.

The apostle says about himself in his last days "*I have finished the race, I have kept the faith. Finally, there is laid up for me the crown of righteousness*" (2 Tim. 4:7-8).

He also says to the Colossians "*to present you holy, and blameless in His sight if indeed you continue in the faith, grounded and steadfast, and are not moved away from the hope of the gospel*" (Col. 1:23).

11. To Be Firm In Faith

Saint Peter the apostle says about the devil's wars "*Resist him, steadfast in the faith* " (1 Pet. 5:9).

12. To Be Rich With Faith

Saint James the apostle says "*Has God not chosen the poor of this world to be rich in faith and heirs of the kingdom which He promised to those who love Him?*"(James 2:5).

13. To Be Filled In Faith

It was said about Stephen "*they chose Stephen, a man full of faith and the Holy Spirit...And Stephen, full of faith and power, did great wonders and signs among the people*" (Acts 6:5,8).

The following qualities are said to be indispensable to faith.

14. Faith Working In With Love

Saint Paul the apostle says "*For in Christ Jesus neither circumcision nor uncircumcision avails anything, but faith working through love.*" (Gal. 5:6), may be he mentioned the expression 'working faith' because faith without deeds is dead (James 2:20). And the expression 'love' is connected with the whole law and the prophets (Matt.22: 40).

There is a great kind of faith:

15. Faith That Performs Miracles

The Lord spoke about "*signs will follow those who believe:*" (Mark 16:17), and Saint James the apostle said "*And the prayer of faith will save the sick*" (James 5:15).

The Peak of this matter is clear in the Lord's saying "*All things are possible to him who believes*" (Mark 9:23).

16. Faith Of Confidence And Believing

It is what the Lord used to ask for from those whom a miracle happened to them. And sometimes He asked "do you believe?". He asked the blind men who asked Him to heal them "*Do you believe that I am able to do this?*" (Matt. 9:28).

The Lord blessed this kind of faith, as well as He said to the Canaanite woman *"great is your faith!* " (Matt. 15:28), and also to the centurion *"I have not found such great faith, not even in Israel!"*(Matt. 8: 10).

17. The Whole Faith

Saint Paul the apostle says "*Though I have all faith, so that I could move mountains ...* " he considered that this faith that moves mountains is the whole faith, that is, its peak and nothing beyond it.

KINDS OF FAITH

There is a great difference between two kinds of faith: theoretical faith and practical faith.

1. The Theoretical Faith

It is an intellectual or philosophical faith. It is just the intellectual conviction in the existence of God and in the existence of unseen matters without their influence on life. There is a saying that proves that the devils have this kind of faith. Then Saint James says about the dead faith, which is with no deeds "*You believe that there is one God. You do well. Even the demons believe--and tremble!*" (James 2:19). The book of Job gives us an evidence to that point because the conversation between God and Satan proves this theoretical faith, then Satan says to the Lord "*Does Job fear God for nothing? Have You not made a hedge around him, around his household, and around all that he has on every side? You have blessed the work of his hands, and his possessions have increased in the land. But now, stretch out Your hand and touch all that he has, and he will surely curse You to Your face!*" (Job 1:9-11). When Satan took permission from God to act, he went to work against Job, and in the second time Satan told the Lord "*Stretch out Your hand now, and touch his bone and his flesh, and he will surely curse You to Your face!*" (Job 2:5).

Hence Satan believes theoretically that, that is God, and that He is the one who blessed the work of Job, and He is able to strike what he has, and to strike his flesh and bones. Every expression coming out of Job against God is considered a curse towards God. Never the less Satan was fighting the kingdom of God and God's children, and he still does.

The theoretical faith of Satan which Job spoke about is a dead faith according to what the apostle said "*Faith without works is dead*" (James 2:20). Thus if faith without deeds is dead, then what is the faith that is loaded with bad deeds opposing every goodness.

The theoretical faith is easy. How easy is it to prove the existence of God with the intellectual proofs and the many evidences, the most important is however the practical faith.

This leads us to the important kind of faith

The Practical Faith

It is the faith, which signs show in the practical life, the life of a believer believing that God is in front of him, he sees and feels Him, and he acts worthy of this faith.

He loves this God who he believes in His existence, His care, His protection, and he talks to this loving God through his prayers and his imploring, and he fears to do anything that may hurt His loving heart... and in tranquillity in His actions, he does not fear and does not trouble, but lives in perpetual peace, he yields his whole life to His wise disposal.

In this way, faith leads the believer to many uncountable virtues.

This kind of faith is the subject of this book, as we will as to describe how faith leads our whole life to become
a life of faith.

This understanding takes us to another quality in the qualities of the true faith:

2. Perpetual Faith

We mean by that, that it does not have occasions. Our faith does not only appear when being in church, or in a spiritual meeting, or when praying, or when reading the Bible, or when having communion; but this faith is apparent at any time and in any place, outside the church as well as inside. God is always in front of us and is always on our minds with faith that does not change. He is not only the Lord of churches or the Lord of the

Bible but He is the Lord of the heart and the mind together and the Lord of life.

3. Faith Without Seeing

This faith does not depend on the senses and is consistent with what the Lord said "*Blessed are those who have not seen and yet have believed.*" (John 20:29). It is not like the scientists who do not believe in anything unless they get it in their laboratories and convince themselves of it with their eyes and instruments, and not like the Sadducees who denied the existence of the angels, the resurrection and the spirits (Acts 23:8), because they have not seen anything from all that...

4. Faith Of Confidence And Test

It is not faith in God what we read about in the theological books or in the religious institutions, or in the churches and in the Sunday schools with all their kinds.

But it is the faith in God that we test in our lives. We were in companionship with Him, we let Him enter in every detail of our lives, and practically tested what David said "*Oh, taste and see that the Lord is good*" (Ps 34:8). We found that God is wonderful, to the most extent, beyond what the mind can imagine.

Our whole life is fellowship with Christ. We tasted His beauty, His love and His care, we also saw His power and His glory.

We saw how He enters into our problems and solves them in ways that could not have occurred to us before.

Because of our test we gained confidence not built on books, but on what we felt by our hands, that's why our faith is a true faith destined in our hearts.

5. A Strong Faith

It is faith that is able to do anything (Mark 9:23), it can overcome any obstacle, it does not see anything impossible. It was said about Zerubbabel "*Who are you, O great mountain? Before Zerubbabel you shall become a plain!*" (Zech. 4:7).

It is faith that can place its foot in water so as to cross the Red Sea in the days of Moses (Ex. 14:22), and to cross the Jordan river in the days of Joshua (Joshua 3). It can walk inside the great sea or river with waters surrounding it like a gate on its right and on its left without any fear.

It is faith that can strike the rock and water comes out of it (Ex. 17:6). It is faith that walks in the desert without any food or guide collecting its food from the manna descending from heaven day by day (Ex. 16:21) guided by the cloud in the day time and by the fire rod at night (Num 9:15-23).

It is the strong faith which Elijah said through it "*There shall not be dew nor rain these years, except at my word*" (1 Kin 17: 1), and thus "*it would not rain; and it did not rain on the land for three years and six months. And he prayed again, and the heaven gave rain*" (James 5: 17-18), and that is how he could close and open the sky.

There are many examples about this strong faith. There are many other examples of this kind but they appear in another form.

6. Faith Which Is Steady

It is a steady faith and is not at all affected by external circumstances; it believes in God's love either on mount Carmel or on Golgotha.

Abraham believed in the love of God that gave him descendants from Sarah in hopeless circumstances, exactly how he believed in the love of God as He said to him "*Take now your son, your only son Isaac, whom you love, and go to the land of Moriah*" (Gen. 22:2).

Abraham when he raised his hand with the knife to slay his son Isaac did not doubt in the love of God, nor in His timing. His faith was never shaken in God, and not even that he will have descendants from Isaac as many as the stars of the sky and the sand of the sea.

Steady faith does not change according to the external circumstances surrounding it, because its confidence is steady in God, and its peace of heart is not affected by the external circumstances but from God Himself, His love and the truth in His timings.

7. Faith As A Gift

There is normal faith and faith which is considered a gift from the Holy Spirit, and no doubt the latter has a higher degree which overcomes the normal faith.

Saint Paul the apostle, says in his speech about gifts "*There are diversities of gifts, but the same Spirit. ... But the manifestation of the Spirit is given to each one for the profit of all: for to one is given the word of wisdom through the Spirit, to another the word of knowledge through the same Spirit, to another faith by the same Spirit, to another gifts of healings by the same Spirit,* " (1 Cor. 12:4-9).

Faith as being among the fruits of the Spirit is also seen in (Gal.5:22).

It becomes clear that we can not separate the faith from the works of the Holy Spirit; either from the fruits of the Spirit, or from the Spirit's gifts; and each of them has its degree.

8. The Sound Faith

How often do people believe in ideas or beliefs political or social, and their belief gives them a power to carry these ideas out and to transfer them to the minds of the people.

The sound faith that has a spiritual nature and has a deep relationship with God "*exhorting you to contend earnestly for the faith which was once for all delivered to the saints.*" (Jude 3) this pure and virtuous faith. This lets us say that Faith is not just a belief but a life... or it is a life built on belief, or it is an experienced belief lived by the people and not just ideas in books.

What we want to speak about in this book is this life, the life of faith.

CHAPTER 4

THE RELATIONSHIP OF FAITH WITH PEACE AND FEARLESSNESS

From the qualities of the believer it is his heart that is full of peace and tranquillity. He does not trouble at all, does not agitate, and does not fear because he believes in God's protection. The believer keeps his inner peace whatever the external circumstances seem to be disturbing.

The person, who feels that he stands alone, fears. He who believes that God is with him does not fear.

1- David the prophet says, "*Though an army may encamp against me, My heart shall not fear; Though war should rise against me, In this I will be confident.*" (Ps 27:3) and if you ask him about the reason in this attitude, then he answers in the same Psalm "*The Lord is the strength of my life; Of whom shall I be afraid?*" (Ps 27: 1). David experienced God, His help and His protection. When evil men advanced towards him to devour his flesh he said "*When the wicked came against me ...They stumbled and fell.*" (Ps 27:2).

He does not receive his tranquillity from the amelioration of the external circumstances surrounding him, but he

receives his tranquillity from God's work in these circumstances and in him.

Consequently David says in the psalm of the shepherd "*Yea, though I walk through the valley of the shadow of death, I will fear no evil; For You are with me*" (Ps 23:4).

If you have this faith, that God is with you, you shall not fear even if an army besieges you, or if war breaks against you, and even if you walk in the valley of the shadow of death.

2- Perhaps We Could Also See This Peace And Fearlessness In The Meeting Of Elijah The Prophet With Ahab.

Ahab the king, was searching for Elijah the prophet everywhere so as to kill him, and in spite of that Elijah went to stand before Ahab. When Obadiah warned Elijah of the danger Elijah answered "*As the Lord of hosts lives, before whom I stand, I will surely present myself to him today*" (1 Kin 18: 15), and the meeting took place. Elijah met Ahab the king and was not afraid of him. Elijah even rebuked him for following the Baals (1 Kin 18:18). Elijah did not fear due to his belief of standing in front of the Lord of armies.

3-The Same Way, We See The Encounter Between David And The Mighty Goliath.

David, the young man, was from faith, full of peace and not fearing Goliath. He even spoke in confidence and told Saul the king "Let no man's heart fail because of him; your servant will go and fight with this Philistine" (1 Sam. 17:32). As for the king and his whole army they were afraid and very frightened, because they were not looking to God who is unseen, as David was... but were concentrating their eyes on what they saw in front of them "a champion " who was "*Six cubits and a span. He had a bronze helmet on his head, and he was armed with a coat of mail, and the weight of the coat was five thousand shekels of bronze.*" (1 Sam. 17:4-7).

David the man of faith, when he entered the field of war he let God enter with him, and he entered the spirit of faith and peace to the hearts of the men of war with his saying "*Who is this uncircumcised Philistine, that he should defy the armies of the living God?... Let no man's heart fail because of him; your servant will go and fight with this Philistine*" (1 Sam, 17:26,32), and he told the Philistine "*You come to me with a sword, with a spear, and with a javelin. But I come to you in the name of the Lord of hosts, the God of the armies of Israel*" (1 Sam. 17:45), that means: you come to me with seen matters and I come to you with who is unseen.

We will notice that the name of God did not part from David's tongue and it granted him peace.

With this faith, peace of heart and confidence, David advanced towards this Philistine and told him with total confidence in faith "*This day the Lord will deliver you into my hand... for the battle is the Lord's*" (1 Sam. 17:46,47).

Really the person who believes does not know any fear whatever the circumstances surrounding him were. His peace of heart does not leave him, but faith grants him courage and bravery.

4-In The Midst Of Distress, Whatever Kind It Is, We See Faith Giving Peace.

A distress can be solved in two ways: one is with faith and the other without. A non believer is troubled, afraid and worried, he imagines the worst results, and thinking disturbs him... but the believer accepts it with tranquillity and with a wonderful peace of heart. Some may ask him about his feelings regarding this distress and he answers "God will interfere in this problem and solve it and it will be for the good". You may ask him how God will interfere, and how God is going to solve it, and he answers: I do not know, and I am not interested, but I know that we do not have to take care of our problems because God takes care of everything.

Really, I do not know how the problem will be solved but I know God who will solve it.

Thus, faith leads the believer to tranquillity. That's how the children of God always live in peace and even in joy, feeling that God is with them and that He takes care of all their matters, and He does for them what they can not do for themselves.

5-Jonah, Being In The Whale's Stomach, Did Not Lose Faith And Peace.

He even prayed to the Lord when he was in the whale's stomach, a prayer full of faith, and he said in confidence "*I will look again toward Your holy temple.*" (Jon. 2:4). He made the Lord a vow and said "*With the voice of thanksgiving; I will pay what I have vowed. Salvation is of the Lord*" (Jon. 2:9).

Even from inside the whale, he saw the Lord's salvation, getting out of the whale, the holy temple and his sacrifice to the Lord and the fulfilling of his vows.

It is faith the source of all peace and ease, no fear in it and no trouble.

6-When Faith Decreases, Then The Person Fears.

Peter in his faith, could walk with the Lord on the water forgetting all the laws of gravitation. When he remembered them and became afraid, he began to sink. The Lord rebuked him saying "*O you of little faith, why did you doubt?*" (Matt. 14:31).

That way, the Lord related fear, doubt and little faith together. It is really a wonderful relation: doubt weakens the faith, a weak faith leads to fear, and fear causes the fall.

In the same manner we speak about the disciples when waves covered the ship they were on. Their sight of the agitated waves covering the ship while the Lord was asleep, made them doubt the Lord's care for them. Doubt weakened their faith and so they became frightened, that is why the Lord rebuked them saying "*Why are you fearful, O you of little faith?*" (Matt. 8:26).

Every time you are afraid, rebuke your self for your little faith. Tell yourself 'where is my faith that God exists and that He controls everyone and sees everything. And where is my faith in God's love, and in His interference in my problems, and in His ability to do everything, and where is my faith in that God does benevolences, and that no doubt He'll do me good?'

All these ideas strengthen your faith and grant you peace and confidence in God's work.

Faith rests the soul, because he who believes in the existence of God does not feel lonely, but has confidence that there is a power beside him.

He believes in the existence of this power that is able to do everything, which is all love and justice, and that can support him. This power works for the best of all and has mercy on all who are in distress. If the believer has confidence in this Godly power then his heart is filled with peace, would not fear and would not be troubled. The non believer on the other hand, tires and stands alone in his distress losing the peace because he does not have confidence in this unseen supporting power.

7-Saint Peter Was In Prison And He Had A Deep Sleep.

King Herod, so as to please the Jews, had James the brother of John, one from the twelve disciples, put to death. He seized Saint Peter also and put him in prison "*delivered him to four squads of soldiers to keep him* ", He intended to kill him after the Passover (Acts 12:1-4).

In spite of being in prison, with the strong guards, and the expectation of being killed... Peter slept, having confidence in the existence of a Godly guardian that guards him more than the soldiers around him. It was a deep sleep, even when the angel came to rescue him he struck Peter on the side to wake him up (Acts 12:7).

What kind of peace of heart is that, that lets a person sleep in such conditions when being imprisoned, and in that same night King Herod was intending to kill him.

It is faith in God's care if God wanted him to live, or faith in a happy eternity if God wanted him to die as a martyr.

In both cases the matter needs to be joyful. That is why peace was filling Peter's heart. He was sleeping calmly and the external matters did not bother him.

Maybe there was another reason for Peter's peace and that is "*Peter was therefore kept in prison, but constant prayer was offered to God for him by the church.*" (Acts 12: 5).

The believer is he who can sleep in God's embrace and rest. He yields his life and all his troubles to God, and he says to God: as long as you have received these matters so I will not trouble myself with them. For me the matter is finished and is transferred into your hands and I have confidence that You will do the best out of it. I sleep and rest and You will give me sleep *"He gives His beloved sleep he loves"* (Ps 127:2).

8-Daniel The Prophet And The Three Young Men As An Example Of Faith Full Of Peace.

Daniel was awaiting to be thrown in the lions' den, and in spite of that he did not lose his peace and his courage. He kept his faith and he prayed to God the Lord, with strength and without fear.

In the lions' den, Daniel's heart was stronger than the hearts of all the lions that were with him, as if he were saying: what if they threw me in the den? Is not God also there, or is not His angel there who could close up the mouths of the lions?

Also the three young men they did not fear the fire.

No doubt, faith creates all courage and bravery in the heart and it takes away all fear.

9-The Same Were The Saints On Their Way To Martyrdom.

They were singing songs of joy and were praising God on their way to death. Neither death nor suffering did trouble them. Their faith was in the other life, in a happy eternity, and in fellowship with God in Paradise. All this filled them with peace and joy and were even looking forward to death, singing with Paul the apostle "*refresh my heart in the Lord*" (Phil. 20).

Death does not frighten the believer but delights him.

10-In Every Distress, Obstacle And Difficulty The Believer Does Not Fear And Does Not Lose His Peace.

A believer overcomes obstacles without fearing them. He feels that God will solve the problems that come across him and that God shall not leave him alone in the problems.

But for the non believer, the problems cause him reluctance and fear, and by his unbelief he becomes a coward. The non-believer may even imagine difficulties and intimidations that do not exist as if "*There is a lion in the road! A fierce lion is in the streets!*" (Prov. 26:13).

A believer does not fear at all whatever troubles and difficulties face him. He faces them with calmness and security having confidence in God's work with him.

11-With Faith, People Preached About Jesus In Countries Where Human Flesh Was Eaten And They Did Not Fear.

They entered unexplored Africa and in the jungles, and in dangerous areas from weather conditions, nature and habits of their people and they did not fear. Their belief in God the protector, gave them power and courage. Also their faith in the goodness and importance of their work; importance of bringing the words of God to the souls there, so that these souls won't perish in non faith. God gave them power and took away the fear from their hearts so they accomplished their work. They did not mind the emigration, nor the cruelty of the weather, nor the barbarity of the people, nor the venturous weather.

12-By Faith, Noah Took Animals With Him On The Ark Without Fear.

As God told Noah to take animals with him two by two so he did. God who gave the order kept Noah safe from them. They were with Noah as they were with Adam in Paradise, to live with them without fear and with peace in the heart, and so it was.

Noah had faith in God's word to him so he did not fear.

13-He Who Believes In An Idea, Faith In It Will Give Him Power To Carry It Out.

That was how the reformers were in all times and places. They believed in an idea so they endeavoured with all strength to carry it out. Because of their faith, they endured many troubles until they completed their work.

Gandhi for example, believed in the person's right in freedom, and he believed in a policy without violence. This faith gave him a wonderful power with which he liberated India, and gave rights to the opposers whereby they obtained equal rights. He was able to endure so that his followers would not face violence, and so that they don't accept violence. His faith in the idea gave him the power to carry it out. How greater it is then to believe in God!

14-Even Faith In Science Does Miracles, An Example To That Are The Astronauts.

I mean by that, what was being told to them about the non gravity area, and how a person can walk in this area without falling. Who has the courage to walk in the atmosphere without fearing? What made the astronauts carry it out was their faith in the scientists' research. Faith gives power and courage. How it is then to have faith in God!

The difference between the most courageous people and the most fearful is faith.

The courageous person, is he who has faith that no harm will happen to him, or that he believes in his work and its necessity whatever happened to him, or that he believes in the quality of courage and fearlessness. However, the coward is the total opposite of that.

15-Faith In Eternity Gives A Person Peace And Ease.

He has confidence that he will obtain his right if not on earth then in heaven, and that he will not be oppressed either here or there. This is also how he will obtain his full joy: what has not come true on earth will surely come true in the eternal paradise. That is how he lives at ease even if he was like poor Lazarus.

16-Faith In The Power And The Sign Of The Cross Prevents Fear.

He who believes in the cross, the sign of the cross, and the power of the cross feels tranquil as he protects himself behind the cross.

If he is faced with fear or danger and he made the sign of the cross his heart will be filled with peace. He will also feel that a power protects him and this power prevents fear from him. He feels that a power has entered his heart which was not there before. The sign of the cross became a weapon for him.

Another person has a great faith in the effectiveness of the psalms. He reads them at any time or in time of need and he feels that the psalm has a special power that eases his heart and grants him peace. If he was afraid and read Psalm 91 (he who dwells in the shelter of the Most High), or 23 (the Lord is my shepherd), or 27 (the Lord is my light and my salvation) ... he feels immediately peace inside him and that the psalm's power has descended upon him.

We know that the psalms were written through the Spirit (Matt. 22:43-44). As a book from the Bible David wrote them lead by the Holy Spirit (2 Pet. 1:21). That is why it has without any doubt, power.

Others have faith in the spirits of the saints and the work of these spirits for them.

Accordingly, they feel peace when they ask for a prayer or help of a certain saint they love and they have confidence in the saints intercession with God.

I remember, in this occasion, an Ethiopian monk who was living in a cave in Natroun valley. Once he got lost during the night as he was complaining of weakness in the eyes. Night and darkness fell upon him. So he drew a large circle on the desert land and surrounded it with the sign of the cross at all sides and he then slept inside it. In the morning, he saw traces of foxes and animals outside the circle; they could not enter the circle to harm him.

I remember some time ago, I was travelling on a ship. The waves became agitated and the passengers were afraid. I looked and I saw among the passengers, a very good person. I had much confidence in his holiness so my heart was rested. I said to myself "it is impossible that God allows the ship to sink and this good person, who loves God, is on board". Yes, the ship was rescued and no harm happened.

It was just the existence of this person as a cause of peace and to strengthen the faith. Maybe, that was also the feeling of other passengers.

There are many uncountable experiences and stories that strengthen the faith but I do not have the capacity to mention them all here.

However what I have mentioned is sufficient for this chapter and now we may enter another sign of the signs of faith.

CHAPTER 5

THE RELATIONSHIP OF FAITH WITH PURITY OF THE HEART

No doubt you are ashamed to err in front of an innocent person you respect.

You may be very cautious in his presence and are ashamed to commit anything terrible in front of him. You don't like that he takes a bad impression about you, or that you fall lower in his eyes You even take care not to err in front of any of your servants or chiefs lest they contempt you, or even lessen their respect of you.

Consequently most of the sins are committed in secret either because of fear or shame. It was said about the sinners that they "*loved darkness rather than light, because their deeds were evil*" (John 3:19). The Lord said about His enemies who conspired against Him "*This is your hour, and the power of darkness*" (Luke 22:53).

If you shame yourself or fear from a person who sees you, so how is it then in the presence of God?

If you completely believed that God is present in every place you are, He sees you, hears you and watches over you, no doubt you will be ashamed or afraid to commit anything wrong in front of God. That is why, when Joseph was offered the sin he refused it saying "*How then can I do this great wickedness, and sin against God?*" (Gen.39: 9).

He considered it wrong against God to break His commandments and it is disrespectful to God, if he did evil in front of Him without bashfulness. Do you have these feelings? Do you place God in front of you in every sin you fight to do? Do you remember what the Lord said to each of the angels of the seven churches (Rev.)? He told each of them "***I know your deeds***" (Rev. 2:2,9,13,19 & Rev. 3:1,8, 1 5).

If you knew this you will be ashamed, afraid and will refrain from sin because the fear of God will always be in front of your eyes every time you try to do wrong.

You will even feel ashamed from the spirits of the angels and saints.

If you believe, from all your heart, that God's angels roam around us (Ps 34:7) and that we "*made a spectacle to the world, both to angels and to men.*" (1 Cor. 4:9) then you will, no doubt, be ashamed of yourself from the angels around you. He will not bear to see your sins due to his holiness, so he will leave you... You no doubt will be ashamed of yourself from the spirits of the saints, your relationships and acquaintances... with this shame you will part from sin and approach the life of purity.

If you believe that God is holy, you will be apprehensive to show your uncleanliness in front of this unlimited holiness. Every time you say 'holy, holy, holy' in your prayers you will feel disgrace in your heart due to your past, and you will not venture to commit any sin in the future. When Isaiah the prophet, heard the seraphim glorify the Lord with this Hymn "*Holy, holy, holy*" he cried out "*Woe is me, for I am undone! Because I am a man of unclean lips*" (Is 6:2-5).

If you believe that God is the examiner of hearts and reader of minds and that He knows all that goes on in your mind and heart with respect to feelings, plans and plots, then you will be afraid of His knowing your inside. You will be ashamed from His Holiness and by leaving these ideas and feelings you will reach the life of purity.

May be you will say: I believe in all these; that God exists, that He sees and hears everything, that He examines hearts and reads minds... and in spite of that I am still in sin... And I answer you: **may be you believe in all these theoretically but you don't live a life suitable to your faith!**

He who lives this faith that God sees him, the angels see him, the spirits see him... If he practically puts this idea in his heart he will be ashamed, his soul will lessen in his own eyes, and he will not dare to continue committing sins. According to one of the fathers every sin is preceded by lust, negligence or forgetfulness.

Maybe the person, during sin, forgets God and His kingdom. Maybe he also forgets that he is created in the image and the likeness of God, if he really believed in that. Maybe he is also forgetful of all God's commandments and warnings although theoretically, he believes in all that but he does not live it. He, as we have already said, has the name of a believer but not the life of one.

Consequently, if you believe in eternity then put it in front of you so as not to err.

He who believes that the day of the Lord will come like a thief (1 Thes. 5:2), that God is just, that He'll give everyone according to what he has done (Rev. 22:12), and he who believes in life after death, judgment, repentance, punishment, standing before God in that day when the books will be opened, that ideas and wishes will be revealed, and the works of everyone will be declared in front of all... he who believes in all that, with a practical faith, it will be difficult for him to err but will find a restraint inside him which dissuades him, fearfully and shamefully... and you see him looking forward to meeting God on that day.

Why do I speak about Eternity, I could say from another point of view: **If you believe in God's love you will be ashamed to hurt His love.**

Many times you say, "God is love" (1 John 4:8,16). During sin you are not in a state of practical faith in His love, or may be this love is not at all in your mind. If you really believe that love is the holy bondage that binds you with God, how will you err? "*Whoever has been born of God does not sin*" (1 John 3:9).

You will not err if you believe in virtue as a way of life. Many speak about virtue. They invite others to it and glorify it a lot. But they do not live it. They do not practically believe that virtue can be their way of life. If they practically believed in that, then they would have lived a pure life and reproved themselves for their weaknesses.

He who also believes in the evanescence of the world will renounce it and will not err.

As David the prophet, said "*I am a stranger in the earth; Do not hide Your commandments from me.*" (Ps 11 9:19), "*For I am a stranger with You, A sojourner, as all my fathers were.*" (Ps 39:12). That's how the men of faith lived "*they were strangers and pilgrims on the earth. ... they desire a better, that is, a heavenly country.*" (Heb. 11:13,16). They renounced everything in this world and obeyed the apostle's saying, "*Do not love the world or the things in the world. And the world is passing away, and the lust of it*" (1 John 2:15, 17).

With this faith, they lived in the world without that the world living in them.

They were those "*And those who use this world as not misusing it.*" (1 Cor. 7:31). With this faith - on a larger scale - lived the monks, hermits, and he mountain inhabitants in devotion and seclusion "*Of whom the world was not worthy. They wandered in deserts and mountains, in dens and caves of the earth.*" (Heb. 11:38).

This is how faith purifies the heart. As the apostle said "*And **this is the victory that has overcome the world--our faht** ."* (1 John 5:4). Our faith, that we live on earth "*while we do not look at the things which are seen, but at the things which are not seen. For the things which are seen are temporary, but the things which are not seen are eternal.*" (2 Cor. 4:18). Yes, faith in the evanescence of the world lets us overcome it and to become purified from it and what it contains.

Faith in eternity gives the person wakefulness in his conscious. This is how the person will always have a living conscious: to judge every work, not only according to success or failure, or according to its results in our lives... but to judge the matters according to eternity... because every thing he does has an effect on his eternal destiny and may be on the destiny of others... every good he does is kept for him in Heaven, but he will have to give an account of every wrong he does to people or to himself on the judgment day.

Faith in the existence of God in front of us gives the heart humility.

It grants the person humility in the heart and in action, and it grants him fear and solemnity because he stands before God. As it was said about Saint Peter during fishing (after the resurrection of Christ) when he knew that the Lord came "*He put on his outer garment for he had removed it*" (John 21:7).

In the presence of the Lord, every person stands in solemnity. According to the person's feeling in the existence of God is his measure of solemnity. That is how people differ one from the other in their feelings during prayer, there are those who kneel and those who prostrate in front of God's unlimited greatness... but he who sits during prayer, what can I say about him?

The perpetual feeling that God exists - even not during prayer - makes the person humble because majesty is only to God alone haughtiness of a person is against faith.

Thus, we see angels in this perpetual solemnity.

The Bible says about the seraphim "*each one had six wings: with two he covered his face, with two he covered his feet, and with two he flew.*" (Is 6:2). If the seraphim covers his face and feet in the presence of God due to His beautiful majesty, then what shall we say? And how shall we be solemn and humble in front of Him?

To this degree we see faith purifying the heart and granting it fear, bashfulness and humility.

He who believes in God's importance to him will fear to err wrong, because it is separation from God. How dangerous is it to a person to be separated from God.

As for he who does, not believe in the danger of sin, and the danger in its spiritual results, becomes lenient with it, falls, and loses his purity. See to what extent the feelings of David were concerning the danger of sin when he told the Lord "*Against You, You only, have I sinned, And done this evil in Your sight*" (Ps 51:4). See also Joseph, he believed that if he did anyone wrong then it was against God (Gen. 39:9).

All these spiritual feelings either they prevent the person from sin like Joseph, or they cause a contrite heart like that of David's. Both are signs of purity of heart.

✣✣✣

CHAPTER 6

SIMPLICITY OF FAITH

Simplicity of faith; many intellectuals seek it but do not find It. Once a philosopher passed by a simple peasant who was praying with strong ardour while kneeling down in solemnity. The peasant was talking to God with persistence and familiarity as if he was standing before Him. The philosopher then said; "I am ready to give up all my philosophy, in return that I acquire something of the faith of this simple man who talks with all this confidence to whom he does not see."

The philosopher felt that this simple man possessed something very precious that with all his philosophy he could not obtain.

Simplicity of faith "believes everything" concerning God and accepts it without investigation or argument, being the argument which the intellectuals are famous for.

This simplicity reminds us of the faith of children who believe in theological and spiritual facts. They have the confidence that does not doubt or lie and does not oppose the mind. Maybe that is one of the reasons that made Jesus tell His disciples "*Unless you are converted and become as little children, you will by no means enter the kingdom of heaven."* (Matt. 18:3). The faith of an adult may be deeper, but the faith of a child is more innocent, simple and sincere; true faith has no doubt in it. May your faith be strong like that of a child's.

I do not agree with those who say that children are non-believers. Paul the apostle, tells his disciple Timothy "*From childhood you have known the Holy Scriptures, which are able to make you wise for salvation through faith which is in Christ Jesus.*" (2 Tim. 3: 15). How great was the praise of Jesus to the child He set in the middle of the disciples (Matt. 18:2,3).

He who follows the simplicity of faith, lives far from the complications of the mind, and lives far from what the mind presents from doubts, thoughts, and may be even misleading. Really, the mind's balance is from God but it may err if separated from faith.

Faith is a kind of splendour God presents to the mind so as to enlighten it.

If the mind stands alone it troubles its owner with ideas. If David, the young man, depended only on his mind and thoughts, he would have feared Goliath. Saul and his army did, but David depended on the simple faith, according to what he told Goliath "*This day the Lord will deliver you into my hand*" (1 Sam. 17:46). However, how did God give them all in their hands? David did not think of that but left it to God Himself because war is to God (1 Sam. 17:46). This is faith. With it David won the war even more than those who used their minds as to balance the matters.

Simple faith is a matter of confidence and not a matter of thinking.

Even if the mind said that war searches for the balance of powers and how one side will overcome? The answer is simple: if God entered the battle He would change the human idea of the balance of power, and David with God's power will be much stronger than Goliath without this balance of power. Here we see that faith - with its simplicity - does not contradict the mind and its balances.

He who lives in simple faith lives without anxiety because anxiety usually comes because of much thinking or that a person thinks about problems in an intellectual way. But in the simplicity of faith the person does what he can and leaves the more important point to God Himself and is not anxious. His confidence that God works for him gives him peace of heart and does not allow anxiety to overcome his feelings.

He who has this simple faith is not anxious because he leaves God the control of his matters. If he has confidence in the good care of God in his life, so he won't worry about tomorrow, because the God of tomorrow will take care of it, and he will welcome everything that happens in his life with the expression "*All things work together for good to those who love God*" (Rom. 8:28).

But he who places his thinking in place of the Godly arrangement will tire a lot and carry his anxieties instead of letting God carry them for him.

The confidence of simple faith in granting prayers, takes away anxiety.

Maybe you all know the story of this village that suffered from dryness. The people of the village decided to set a prayer day so that God causes rain to fall. All went to pray and a young girl went carrying an umbrella. When they asked her about the reason, she said: "aren't we praying because of rain? What shall we then do when God hears our prayers and it starts to rain and we don't have any umbrellas?" She had faith that God will grant their prayer. And because of her faith it did rain.

This simple faith has its strength regarding miracles and visions. A miracle can happen to a person and not to another, because the former, in his simple faith, believes and accepts it. But for the latter, the difficulties that his mind presents, make him doubt inside himself about its ability to happen.

The same also happens concerning visions. Some see the Godly visions by their simple faith, and others do not owing to the complications of their minds. This is very clear as it happened during the appearance of the Virgin Mary in her church in Zeitoun, Cairo.

The mind tries to analyse everything scientifically or else it will not believe. As for faith, it needs belief, in simplicity, far from the complications of their minds.

That's why miracles and visions happen mostly to simple people. But for most intellectuals, who disapprove of them and who mock their believers, it rarely happens to them whether to bring them to faith or so that they are a witness of them (John 15:22).

Even the Jews did not believe the miracle of the man who was born blind and said that he who healed him was a sinner (John 9:24). The mind put the problem of healing on a Sabbath in front of them, so that they lost faith (John 9:16).

That is why Jesus said of those and praised the simple ***"I thank You, Father, Lord of heaven and earth, that You have hidden these things from the wise and prudent and have revealed them to babes.*** " (Matt. 11:25). With the word *babes,* He meant the simple faith. But those wise and learned in this verse are those who are proud of their knowledge and understanding, and who only depend on their minds far from faith, even some of the spiritual men admitted in sorrow and said: "this is the fruit which Adam and Eve ate from". they meant by that, the knowledge away from God.

One of the nights I was coming back after visiting one of the fathers in the mountni . Darkness was already spreading and it was told to me "don't come back alone to the monastery so that you don't get lost". I knew the way quite well and I believed in God's guidance and in spite of that I said "If I get lost then I'll spend the night in the desert till morning." I had faith in my depth in God's protection, especially that many bedouins spend the nights in the desert without fear, but it was told to me "you are more simple than usual, and you don't know the mountain. Because the mountain is full of insects, bears and there is also the danger of fierce animals and other weather conditions. The mind was always talking in my ears to remove what I had in my heart from simple faith. I came back at that same night to the monastery with one of the fathers. My mind did not give me at that time any chance to experience the work of God with those who walk at night in the desert. Or even, to experience the faith of the bedouin who spends each night there, and the care and protection of God is with him.

I thank God that He compensated me for that later on when I lived alone in the mountain.

The mind can imagine danger everywhere and at the same time does not give the thinking a chance in God's work. On the contrary, it causes the non believer to be afraid.

That does not mean that a person throws himself in jeopardy without wisdom. If a person was as cautious as can be and then found himself in a so called 'danger' then with all simplicity he will have confidence in God's protection and care, and sings with the prophet David "*A thousand may fall at your side, And ten thousand at your right hand; But it shall not come near you.* " (Ps 91:7).

Simple faith has confidence that God's hand will interfere to rescue and solve any problem.

The person believes totally that God, as a lover of human beings, and doer of benevolences, will no doubt interfere in the problem according to His promise to His children and He'll spread His hands to solve it.

But how does this happen? Simple faith does not ask that.

He accepts the work of grace in simplicity without investigating how it works.

How many times did we try to solve our problems with human methods and all these ways failed and did not have any results. The fingerprints of God were clear beyond all thinking.

Simple faith has confidence in God's work, by belief and experience.

Faith brings the person to trials. Tests deepen the faith and build it on firm basis and not on theoretical ones. Faith and trials strengthen one another until the person reaches conviction and simplicity of faith.

Simple faith has confidence that everything is possible and that nothing is impossible.

It has complete confidence that God can do all things and that no plan can be thwarted (Job 42:2), even if it was difficult to understand it happening. The person believes in the Lord's saying "*All things are possible to him who believes.*" (Mark 9:23).

That's why simple faith, is beyond all doubts.

It is a strong faith, stronger than any doubt, because doubts are the work of the mind, and the mind is proud of its measures. But the believer has overcome the stage of the mind and has lived in a higher and deeper level. Higher than the doubts is the simplicity of faith.

Some try to transfer the problem of religion to philosophy and to bring it out of the heart and the soul and restrict it only to the limit of the mind.

That was what Saint Paul the apostle fought with all his might, and said "*Not with wisdom of words, lest the cross of Christ should be made of no effect.*" (1 Cor. 1:17-20)

No doubt, the simple believer who treasures up his faith in himself, above the level of investigation, is stronger in faith than some theologians who acquire their faith from books. They think they have faith. It may be that faith that can be easily shaken by the opposite intellectual thoughts.

Train yourself to the life of simple faith, and make use of the experience that happens in your life or the life of others, and do not let much thinking keep you far from faith.

CHAPTER 7

OBEDIENCE OF FAITH OR A LIFE OF SUBMISSION

He who believes in God's love, His watching over him, His wisdom and handling of his life, and believes that God does benevolence for him, yields his life to God to plan it as God sees fit.

With that conviction, the person will always live in the obedience of faith.

He yields his life to God and he is tranquil and glad. But he who does not live the life of submission is troubled about his life and keeps on thinking: what am I? and how am I? and when am I? is it necessary that I change what I am doing? or shall I stay as I am? Thinking tires him and most probably he loses his peace, and continues in perpetual search and discusses the matters with himself without end. He neither thinks of rest nor leaves the matter to God like the man of faith.

The faithful person, when he yields his life to God does not set any conditions on God, does not ask Him for guarantees and does not observe God in His work with him.

He has full confidence in God, in His love, wisdom and ability. He has faith that God knows what is good for him more than he himself does. That is why he yields his life in His hands and forgets it there.

As long as he has faith in God's work with him, he won't be able to be anxious or interested, and won't tire himself with thinking. The believer lives at peace more than he who thinks for himself and his thinking tires him.

Many do not accept the submission to God unless their human ways fail!

Their principal way is the complete reliance on their human arms either on the esteem of their minds, abilities and tricks, or their getting used to this way, owing to their false belief, or their conviction that a person turns to God only in time of full disability and failure. Then, at that time they come to God because they have tried every trick and method and did not reach their aim, and because their minds have grown tired and exhausted without any use and there was no other way except through God.

This is not faith but it is the pressing necessity to God. Faith is that you seek God in the trivial as well as in big matters.

Jesus said "For without Me you can do nothing." (John 15: 5). That is because every power we have is from Him, even correct thinking, good will and the ability to work. The intelligence on what we depend on is also from Him. How true the saying of the apostle is "*For it is God who works in you both to will and to do for His good pleasure.*" (Phil. 2:13).

Our work in reality is to participate with God in His work for us. This is our participation with the Godly nature, with the Holy Spirit participating with God at work. Just what Saint Paul the apostle, said about himself and his colleague Apollos "*For we are God's fellow workers*" (1 Cor. 3:9).

Every work in which God does not participate in is not a holy or a blessed work. The submission of our will and desire to Him is a kind of participation with Him. We are like tools between His hands doing His will. He conducts it as He wishes. It works with His thinking and wishing, or yielding our will with His will as a companionship of senses with the brain.

The most dangerous thing which can threaten the spiritual life is the person's independence of God.

This is the big sin that King Saul committed so God rejected him (1 Sam. 16). He used to work with his thinking and planning away from God's advice and companionship and didn't see that he is in need to let God participate with him at work, as if he was saying: as long as I can do this work I'll do it with all power and with all haste even without prayer because my will alone will carry it out without depending on God, and if I fail, then I will seek Him! God granted me a mind and will so why don't I use them? There are many like Saul.

God granted humanity the mind and will but not independent of Him

And not that it depends upon itself. The Bible says "*And lean not on your own understanding*" (Prov. 3:5). We remember that the sin of the first human was his attempt to obtain knowledge without God (Genesis 3).

When the human starts to say "I know and I can, so what is the use of God in this matter?" He then becomes separated from the faith of God and enters the faith of ego.

The believer is not only satisfied with the dependence on God but also yields everything to Him.

The believer tells Him: "My life is the work of Your hands and it is now between Your hands, do with it what You want." Where You want me to go I will go and what You want me to be I will be. I don't have a special will, my only wish is that I do Your will and to be one with Your will to want what You want, You the doer of benevolence.

I don't mention anything that I know. Every human's wisdom is foolishness in God's eyes (1 Cor. 1:20). The real wisdom is from You God, alone. You are the wisdom (1 Cor. 1:24). You are "*in whom are hidden all the treasures of wisdom and knowledge.*"(Col.2:3).

I admit that I don't know so I submitted my life in Your hands.

You know good more than I do and You know the good for me more than I do for myself . I have confidence in Your wisdom and in Your planning of my life. Even if You wished me a test or a distress I will accept it from You, considering that it is true good from Your hands. Had it not been for your love for me,

You would not have accepted it for me. Really, in many cases we don't know where the good is!

The life of submission does not know any complaints or murmurs, but accepts everything with satisfaction and gladness.

As long as you have confidence in God's wisdom in His plans for you, then why do you complain, murmur or worry. If murmurs enter your life, this is a good indication which shows that your faith has weakened

He who lives a life of faith and submission lives always in joy and thankfulness.

The believer does not complain but gives thanks. The smile does not leave his lips, cheerfulness does not leave his face and joy does not leave his heart. He believes in God's wisdom and love. He also believes that God's will is always good and useful. He submits to God's will in joy.

He does not submit to God's will due to being obliged or compelled, as if his heart was saying to God "what can I do oh Lord? You are strong and I am weak. All what you do I accept. I am awaiting the end of this matter". No doubt that these thoughts are of a person who is tired within. He speaks with complaining words in a yielding manner. Yielding is not at all like this.

What is then the meaning of "let Your will be done" in the life of faith and submission?

The believer says in complete satisfaction of heart: "God I submit to your will because I like Your will from the depths of my heart and I have confidence in You and in Your will. Your will has corrected my thoughts, my opinions in certain matters, and improved my way of life... how beautiful are your ways Lord "*How unsearchable are His judgments and His ways past finding out!*" (Rom. 11:33). Your will is the most beautiful song on my tongue, and the most beautiful news in my ears. So let your will be done because there is no other will better than that. I feel ignorant beside any will that opposes it, either it is for me or for others."

The life of submission is not submission to the actual matters without conviction!

It is not submission to the policy of a Godly pressure that imposes itself on you and you are obliged to submit to it either you want it or not

No my brothers and sisters, that is not the meaning of the expression "let Your will be done". The life of submission teaches us to feel that God's will is the full benevolence, and that it is the best for us and it is a reason for our joy and cheerfulness. That is why David was singing about God's commands and tells the Lord "your commands are my lesson, Your commands are my pleasure. I meditate on your commands and I learn them" (Ps 119).

Submission to God should be real submission and not only be appearance. Some think that they yield themselves to God although they impose their plans on Him. Every time

God acts in his life he tries to stop God and says, “wait Lord so that I see what You do with me.” This matter is not good.

Do this and that so that I rest. This is how he tries to be a planner, he plans and God does!

No, submission is not like that, but it is that you leave God do what He does, and that you are satisfied with what He does, and that you don't resist God's plans with your actions, and don't resist His plans with what you do according to your wishes.

The believer leaves God the planning and does not accept that he plans for himself.

What was the sin of Adam except that he began to manage himself in obtaining knowledge? How to become like God? How to build himself... that is why he fell.

The sin of Satan was that he began to manage himself, to build and to enlarge as he likes.

“*I will ascend into heaven, I will exalt my throne above the stars of God... I will ascend above the heights of the clouds, I will be like the Most High.*” (Is 14:13-14). They are plans that resemble daydreaming, Satan planned it for himself and he fell.

The same also happened to those who built the tower of Bable. They planned how to build themselves and they failed.

They said “*Let us build ourselves a city, and a tower whose top is in the heavens; let us make a name for ourselves, lest we be scattered abroad over the face of the whole earth.*” (Gen. 11:4). Their planning was against them. What they feared was what happened to them “*The Lord scattered them abroad over the face of all the earth.*” (Gen. 11:9).

The spiritual person does not do that but says in a life of submission “***Unless the Lord builds the house, They labor in vain who build it.***” (Ps 127: 1).

God is he who builds us and not ourselves, so let us yield ourselves to Him so that He builds us.

That is how we live in peace, having confidence in God's work in us and in His successful work. We stand and meditate and see miracles from His planning. Having confidence that He does benevolence whatever happens in front of us which seem to be strange, difficult or against what we hoped for.

It is not important if we understand what God does, but that we accept it with faith and submission.

The Bible is full of examples of submission in the lives of men of faith:

1-Our father Abraham, for example, whose story with God began with God saying to him “*Get out of your country, From your family And from your father's house, To a land that I will show you.*” (Gen. 12: 1).

Abraham neither asked why nor where but he just obeyed.

This is the life of submission that does not argue nor discuss, but accepts and obeys without reluctance. It puts the understanding to the side and concentrates itself on God.

2-That is also how Noah was in the arc, Jonah in the whale's stomach and Moses in the Red Sea a life of complete submission.

It is the obedience of faith. As long as God wants that then we do not discuss with Him. What is our limited and weak mind that we discuss with God the unlimited with full wisdom? Moses, at the beginning of his message, argued with God on how to go to Pharaoh (Ex. 3), but when he grew in faith and submission he did not argue about entering the Red Sea.

3-Saint Mary the Virgin, lived her life as an example of obedience and submission.

With her love of virginity, she was told to get engaged to a man and to live with him in one house and she obeyed. God sent her an angel telling her that she will be pregnant and give birth to a son and she told him "*Behold the maidservant of the Lord! Let it be to me according to your word.*" (Luke 1:38) she gave birth to Jesus, and saw all the miracles that surrounded this birth, and was told to escape to Egypt and she accepted all that in obedience of faith. Also in submission she returned from Egypt and accepted to live in Nazareth (Matt. 2:23), about which it was written that nothing good comes from it (John 1:46).

Her motto in this life of submission was her famous saying “may it be to me as you have said”

4-Faith and submission also appear in the apostles' life in their spontaneous obedience to the Lord's saying “follow me”

This is what the Lord told Matthew (Levi) at the tax collector's booth (Mark 2:14). Matthew did not discuss but “*He left all, rose up, and followed Him.*” (Luke 5: 28) and did not think at all of his responsibilities and work.

The same also happened when the Lord called Peter, Andrew and the rest of the apostles. Peter summarises all the stories of calling in his saying to the Lord “*We have left all and followed You*” (Luke 18:28).

It is the obedience of faith that follows God wherever He goes without question, inquiry or thinking about the future. Everyone obeyed without knowing where he was going to (Heb. 11:8).

How many times are we called by God but we stay in our relaxed perception of our future?

That's why we ask many questions and try to get what we can from guarantees. With all this we get out of faith and become viewers. To the future we see by our own eyes and are relaxed about it, and not to the unknown future that we see through the eyes of faith, and accept it through a life of submission and obedience.

5-Jeremiah the prophet, is an example of a life of faith, submission and obedience.

He followed God, in faith, in ways he never thought he would go through and at the end, he summarised his experience about the life of submission in his deep saying "*O Lord, I know the way of man is not in himself; It is not in man who walks to direct his own steps.*" (Jer. 10:23). Why doesn't he guide his steps? Because it is God who leads and guides these steps.

This is the life of submission that you walk after God and not after your mind.

You walk not according to your wishes and desires and not according to the wishes and/or advice of other people but after God Himself who leads your life. He puts your life at any place and position according to His wisdom. So ask yourself whether God leads your life, or that a certain desire leads it and which guides your actions and foot steps.

6-Joseph is a wonderful example of the life of submission.

God showed him in a vision that he will reign over his brothers, and that they will all bow to him (Gen. 37: 10). How was the promise fulfilled! His brothers took him and threw him in a well to kill him. They then sold him as a slave. The Midianites pulled him out from the well to sell him to the Ishamelites (Gen. 37:28), and then they sold him to Potiphar to serve in his house.

In all that, Joseph did not murmur against God but kept quiet, and submitted calmly to what God allowed to happen and followed in faithfulness and sincerity. He accepted life as a slave. He was content with misfortune but misfortune did not accept him! He was accused of a bad and false charge and was thus thrown in prison as a criminal.

It did not happen that Joseph asked God why and where are Your promises?

He kept quiet in a wonderful example of a life of submission and obedience of faith, and never murmured. The only time he strayed from the life of submission was after explaining a dream to the king's cupbearer he told him "*When it is well with you, and please show kindness to me; make mention of me to Pharaoh, and get me out of this house.*" (Gen. 40:14) When he did that, the spiritual inspiration answered this demand by saying "*Yet the chief butler did not remember Joseph, but forgot him.* " (Gen. 40:23). God did not forget Joseph who stayed in prison in life of submission until He got him out in wonderful glory.

7-David the prophet is also an example who led a life of submission and obedience of faith.

David was taking care of the sheep in the wilderness. God sent Samuel the king, to anoint David a prophet. Samuel did it but did not hand him anything from the kingdom and David kept on caring for the sheep without murmuring. He was then chosen a servant of King Saul who was rejected from God as an evil spirit from the Lord tormented him (1 Sam. 16:14) and David did not reclaim.

He did not say I am the King chosen from God so how can I serve this rejected person? But in a life of submission he accepted this situation and he used to calm King Saul when the devils tormented him. Saul kept on going after David from wilderness to wilderness trying to kill him because he was envious and jealous of him. And it never did happen that David discussed with God or told Him 'where is Your timing? Where is the holy anointment for a great prophet?' He did not say 'what evil have I done so that I deserve all this?' But he waited in calmness and submission for the salvation of God and it happened.

8-The disciples of the Lord are also examples who led a life of submission.

The Lord called them for service as He said to Peter and Andrew "*Follow Me, and I will make you fishers of men* " (Matt. 4:19). Three years passed by and they were still following the Lord without being of service. They did not 'fish' anyone. Then the Lord was crucified and they feared and closed themselves in the upper room so that the Jews would not get them and in spite of all that they did not complain and remained in the life of faith and submission.

When the Holy Spirit ascended on them on Pentecost the Lord fulfilled His promise. In one day Peter could save three thousand souls due to his preaching and if he would have saved two souls a day he would not have come to this total number. The life of submission tells the apostle "*Wait on the Lord; Be of good courage, And He shall strengthen your heart; Wait, I say, on the Lord!*" (Ps 27:14).

Yes Lord I will wait for Your promise to save souls. But do I have three years to wait or more? It is like that but "*it is not for you to know the times or dates the Father has set by His own authority*" (Acts 1:8).

The life of faith does not question the Lord about the range of awaiting His timing.

It does not say to the Lord, why did you Lord make Peter wait more than three years to save souls? And why did you let Abraham wait twenty five years so that Your promise is fulfilled concerning the birth of Isaac? And why did You leave David to be humiliated by Saul ten years until Your promise of becoming a king was fulfilled?

The life of submission does not doubt and sees in a waiting the Godly wisdom.

David was a young boy when he was chosen. Waiting was useful for him till he grew older and mature and so that people's love for him grew day by day. Also, waiting was beneficial for Peter until he completed his discipleship to the Lord and until the Holy Spirit descended over him and the disciples so that they may all gain its power. Also the awaiting of Isaac's birth was beneficial so as to become son of the promised.

9-Of the most beautiful examples of the life of faith is Isaac being presented as a sacrifice.

Abraham was patient for twenty-five years until Isaac was born, his beloved son who took his time. Abraham was completely happy with him. Isaac grew older and then the Lord told Abraham "*Take now your son, your only son Isaac, whom you love, and go to the land of Moriah.*"(Gen. 22:2). Whose heart can bear this? And whose mind can hear that without doubting?

Abraham who led a life of submission did not argue and did not hesitate in carrying it out. But he woke up early the next day and took Isaac to sacrifice him. He did not think to himself more tender than God. He did not doubt at all in God's love and judgement.

Obedience is not only in the simple matters, but appears in its glory in the matters that seem difficult to carry out.

The life of submission appears in entering through the narrow path and the road of agony.

As long as God agrees to this narrow door, so no doubt it will be the best door and we do not discuss it but are happy about it. We say that, through it you test the love of your children and the purity of their hearts and that you prepare crowns for them in Your kingdom.

The martyrs received all kinds of pains in joy with this faith. And all your children Lord "*Count it all joy when you fall into various trials*" (James 1:2).

NOT KNOWING WHERE TO GO TO

1-This is how our Father Abraham followed God to the unknown, not knowing where the road will lead him, but having confidence that God accompanies him through the way and guides his steps.

2-This is also what happened with the pure apostles when the Lord called them and they followed, and they did not know where. At that time, Jesus did not have a known residence and he did not even have a place to rest his head (Luke 9:58). He wandered through the cities and villages teaching and healing in despite not having an official profession in the Jewish society, not having a known income and when He called His disciples He even told them "*Provide neither gold nor silver nor copper in your money belts, nor bag for your journey...*" (Matt. 10:9,10, Mark 6:8).

If one asked one of the disciples at the time: What is your work? What is your future with Christ? He would have stood with a big question mark not knowing any answer, except that of a life of submission. It suffices him that he walks with Christ in spite that in his being with Him and in His presence he does not do anything. Jesus does everything and the disciples are just viewers.

3-Another example is of Saint Mark the apostle, when he entered Alexandria.

He entered it without knowing where to go to as there was no church where he could stay, he did not have people there nor residence. On the contrary, idolatry was everywhere and Judaism was opposing the faith. But Saint Mark came to Egypt with faith and God lead him to Anianos although he did not have this matter at all on his mind.

What happened to Saint Mark happened also to the rest of the apostles. The names and places may have been different but the heart of the subject is the same, as if every apostle was saying: **if the service was a human work it would interest me to know the plan of my way; but if the service is a Godly work so I don't care where I go to as I am with God so I go wherever He guides me.**

4-John the Baptist saw that his duty was to witness the truth. He witnessed the truth and rebuked King Herod saying "you are not justified" and was not interested where it will lead to prison or to death. The message of God was fulfilled in complete obedience of faith. Life and destiny are submitted to God to completion.

This was how Paul the apostle witnessed for the Lord not caring where he got into "trouble or hardship or persecution or famine or nakedness or danger or sword", he says with confidence in the life of submission "*In all these things we are more than conquerors through Him who loved us*" (Rom. 8:35,37).

In all these matters, the children of God walked in the way of life, the life of submission.

All what interests them is that God leads them and they do not care where to. They have confidence in faith, that it will lead them to green pastures and to wells of living waters. Their experience with God makes them happy with His guidance, having confidence in His love.

5-Isaac, the son of Abraham carried wood and went after his father not knowing where they were heading. All what he learned in his life was submission and obedience, and Isaac went with them to the place of where he was to be sacrificed. Abraham tied him up and put him on the altar on top of the wood (Gen. 22) and raised his knife. All this and Isaac was in complete submission. He did not doubt in his father's love nor in the love of God and he always gained.

With his submission, he gained the obedience of faith, his life and God's promises.

6-The servant of Abraham, when he went out to search for a wife for Isaacs did not know where to go to.

He yielded his paths to God to guide him. God planned everything for him in a wonderful way that he stood astonished in front of it. Everything happened according to what Abraham asked him and that's why he said "*Lord has prospered my way*" (Gen 24:56).

As if he was saying "I did not know where I was going to, but I knew exactly that God would be with me"

The same nearly happened to Jacob on his journey to his uncle Laban. How beautiful is the Lord's saying to him "*I am with you and will keep you wherever you go.*" (Gen. 28:15).

7-the Israelites in the wilderness, did they know where they were going to?

They did not know anything. God used to guide them day by day. They would go or stay according to God's guidance. This guidance was in the form of a cloud during the day and a rod of fire in the night. The people were in complete submission to God's guidance not questioning

Moses did not have a plan for his journey nor a map to follow as if he was saying: **it is enough Lord that Your cloud is above our heads and the rod of fire in front of us**. We do not plan our way but Your good will does. We are happy to be under Your guidance. Wherever Your cloud goes we will also go and wherever it stays we will stay under it.

Let the meeting camp in the wilderness move towards the unknown. It is unknown to us but is in Your knowledge since the beginning of time. That suffices us so that we yield ourselves to this unknown, and we have complete confidence that we are on the way to Canaan.

8-Saint Antonious, father of monks, when he entered the desert did not know where he was going just like Saint Paul, the first traveller.

Also all the other travelling Saints and hermits when they entered the unknown wilderness, did not have a certain place in mind to go to. What was in front of them was the spiritual aim to be alone with God in a calm and peaceful life, yielding their lives totally to Him "lost in the pastures, mountains and the earth's cracks".

If you ask anyone of the hermits where they are staying, they would answer, "**On a map I do not know where this place is that I live in but on the map of love I know that I am in the Father's embrace**."

9-Some may ask: shouldn't every one make an estimation of the cost according to the Lord's commandment Himself (Luke 14:28)?

The life of faith is far from the science of mathematics so then what does Saint Luke mean by all this that everyone sits down and estimates the costs of outlays?

The cost of outlay are: Do we have enough faith?

Do you have enough faith that you yield the whole matter to God to manage it? You do what you can but this is the least wanted. The principal point is your faith in what God does and your yielding to Him in the whole matter.

This is our way when we wanted to build a church or any project for service or caring. The main question was not "from where do we pay the costs?" but the main question was, does God agree with this project or not? If He allows it then He will take care of the costs, we only have to start it and God's hand completes the work with us "*Unless the Lord builds the house, They labour in vain who build it*" (Ps 127:1).

Faith is that you close your eyes and look at God.

As long as you open your eyes you will walk with the bodily senses, but if you close this bodily eye you will walk with heart and soul.

If you are convinced with your spiritual senses that God will go with you on your path, walk in it even if it was through the valley of the shadow of death, having confidence that there you will not fear any evil because God is with you (Psalm 23).

10-This is the life of submission, where God chooses for us what we want without choosing ourselves, taking advice from the story of Lot and Abraham.

Lot chose for himself to live in Sodom where the valley was full of tar pits (Gen 14: 10-11) and he knew where he was going to. Abraham did not choose anything for himself, but God told him "*Get out of your country, From your family And from your father's house, To a land that I will show you.* " (Gen. 12: 1) and what was the result? Lot cursed when he was in Sodom and

Abraham saved him (Gen. 14), all his money was burnt and he lost everything there.

The life of submission of Abraham had a better result.

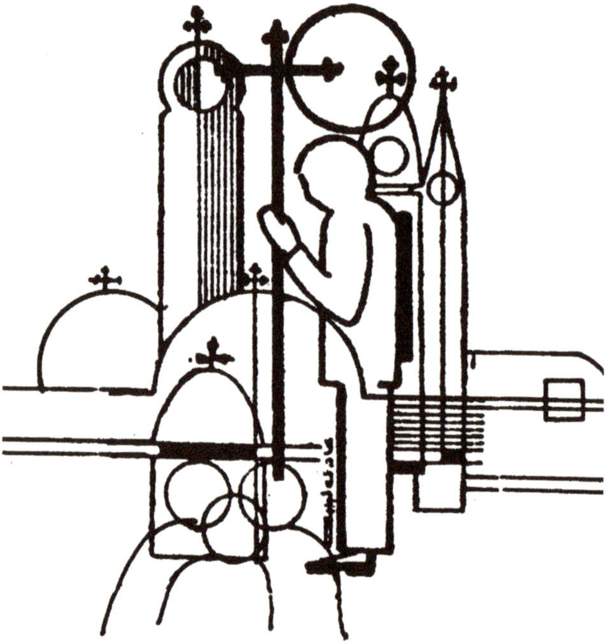

CHAPTER 8

WHAT STRENGTHENS THE FAITH?

Faith is a virtue like all other virtues; it can be strengthened and it can be weakened.

We do not have to only keep our faith, but to also follow all the means that make it grow and increase (2 Thess.1:3 & 2 Cor.8:7). What are the means that strengthen our faith? The means are:

1-Confidence In God's Qualities

a- Always put in your heart that God is a doer of benevolence, so that you can strengthen your faith with His care and protection. Always tell yourself "*All things work together for good to those who love God.*" (Rom. 8:28). Have confidence that everything God does is benevolent, and that everything He allows to happen will no doubt lead to good whatever seems to be the matter. God showed benevolence to Joseph when he was sold as a slave and thrown into prison without any charges. All these distresses were in God's plan for the good of Joseph, and for the good of the whole region. This is what Joseph told his brothers who sold him "*So now it was not you who sent me here, but God.*" (Gen. 45:8), "*You meant evil against me; but God meant it for good, in order to bring it about as it is this day.*" (Gen. 50:20).

b- Have confidence **that God is a father and that He is the Living One**. No doubt, He treats His children with tenderness and gives them good gifts. God said in His fatherly tenderness, that He engraved us on the palms of His hands (Is 49:16). Even if a mother forgot her child, He won't forget us (Is 49: 15). In His fatherhood He gives us all that we need without asking.

c- **What also strengthens the faith is to have confidence in God's ability to do anything**. He loves and wants benevolences for you. He has the ability to do all, in spite of the fact that the matter would seem difficult.

When our father Abraham raised his hand with the knife to sacrifice his only son Isaac, he had faith that God is loving and He inevitably wanted benevolence from all this. According to God's promise Abraham had full faith that he will have as many descendants from Isaac as the stars of the sky.

He even had faith that if Isaac died, then God was able to raise him from the dead and to fulfil His promise. "*That God was able to raise him up, even from the dead.*" (Heb. 11: 19). He is "*A father of many nations in the presence of Him whom he believed--God, who gives life to the dead and calls those things which do not exist as though they did.*" (Rom. 4:17).

Moses entered the Red Sea and crossed it having faith in God's ability to do anything and Joshua entered the Jordan river and also crossed it; each one of them with his people.

d- **Have confidence in the God's judgment**, and that all His planning is for good, even if you don't understand the depth of His judgment.

If you believe in God's judgment, you will live in peace and accept everything with satisfaction. But if your human mind doesn't have confidence in God's judgement you will live in murmur, complaints and psychological weakness. In all that happens to you say to Him; "I have confidence Lord in Your judgement and in Your good planning. And if my understanding is not paralysed, no doubt, I will know later what You meant, just as Joseph did." Have confidence, that God is a doer of benevolence, that He is a loving father, that He is wise in His planning, that He wants good for you and that He is able. All these things deepen your faith and grant you peace of heart.

2- Confidence in the sincerity of God's timing

God promised our father Abram that He will give him descendants, and He did grant him many descendants, although after a long time. He also promised him that his descendants will be as many as the stars of the sky and so it was, although his wife was barren and he was of old age. God also promised His people freedom from captivity and He did free them.

He promised Elijah to help him in the time of famine and He did aid him with a miracle (1 Kin 17:3-6).

God promised our mother Eve that her descendants will crush the head of the serpent (Gen. 3:15); this promise was fulfilled on the cross.

God also promised that He would pour out His Spirit on all people (Joel 2:28), and He did that day on Pentecost and we are still God's temple (1 Cor. 3:16).

All God's promises are sincere. We need them as much as those long ago in history did.

These are everlasting promises from God. These would comfort us when we live in them and in faith, for example, in His saying; "*I am with you always, even to the end of the age.*" (Matt. 28:20), "*For where two or three are gathered together in My name, I am there in the midst of them."* (Matt. 18:20), "*I will give you a mouth and wisdom which all your adversaries will not be able to contradict or resist."* (Luke 21:15), *"Do not worry about how or what you should speak. For it will be given to you in that hour what you should speak; for it is not you who speak, but the Spirit of your Father who speaks in you."* (Matt. 10:19-20), also His saying about the church that the gates of Hell will not overcome (Matt. 16:18).

May we live in these promises with all our hearts, so as to strengthen our faith.

How wonderful it would be if you, dear reader, collect all these promises and read them frequently and tell yourself. No doubt God is sincere in His promises, and consequently with no doubt I have to live happily with these Godly promises. The continuous remembrance of God's promises comforts the soul and strengthens the faith.

3- Look Unto God And Not Unto The Surrounding Circumstances

The surrounding circumstances were calling for hopelessness before crossing the Red Sea. But Moses called the people to look unto God and said to them "*Stand still, and see the salvation of the Lord, which He will accomplish for you ... The Lord will fight for you, and you shall hold your peace.*" (Ex 14:13-14).

The same also happened between David and the mighty Goliath. If David looked to the mighty and challenging Goliath he would have been at a loss. But through faith he looked unto God who will capture him in His hand (1 Sam. 17).

The same situation also happened in the miracle of the five loaves and the two fish. When the disciples saw the existing food and the thousands of people present they said "what is this food to these people?" But Jesus looked up and blessed the food. If the disciples also looked up with faith they would have rested and saw the power of God.

Martha looked at the tomb of her dead brother who died four days back, and said that he smells bad. But the Lord told her haven't I told you that if you believed, you would have seen the glory of God (John 11:39-40).

So we always have to look above so that faith enters our hearts.

We have to look up unto the loving God who is able to do anything, and not to concentrate our thoughts on the surrounding circumstances.

Don't look to the power of your enemies, but look unto God who will rescue you from them.

Don't look at the sin which "*has cast down many wounded, And all who were slain by her were strong men..* " (Prov. 7:26), but look unto the Lord Jesus who "*Will save His people from their sins.*" (Matt. 1:21).

4-The stories of faith and companionship with men of faith.

That's why when God wanted to give lessons about faith He said "*Consider the lilies of the field... even Solomon in all his glory was not arrayed like one of these.*" (Matt. 6:28-29). So if the grass of the field. God clothed it like that, will He not much more clothe you, O you of little faith?

He also said, "look at the birds of the sky" Once I did what the Lord ordered and I looked at a bird in the garden of the monastery with many grains in front of her. She only picked up two or three and left all the rest and flew "She did not store them in a barn" according to what the Lord said. She had confidence that any place she flies to, the Lord will grant her food, so why should she then store grains? Why should she leave the high and the wide sky to stay near the grains to store them just like what the ant does.

The Lord gave us a similar example in the story of the manna and its collecting.

The people used to collect it according to their needs day by day without storing it and those who didn't obey and stored it, the manna became contaminated with "*worms and stank.*" (Ex. 16:20).

Whenever a person reads stories about faith, about the confidence in God and miracles happened with His Saints, his heart will be filled with faith and he will come to love this life full of faith. Also when he associates with men of faith, he will learn to imitate their lives of faith. God's works in their lives will excite him and he will take them as an example. That is why one of the fathers said, "the news of the saints are appetising".

For this reason, the Bible has registered many stories of faith for us to be affected and to learn from them. It will also strengthen our faith, as we see practical examples of the life of faith we desire. We see in front of us the way the men of faith went along, and how God treated them and how they dealt with Him.

If reading affects a person then there is no doubt, their association with someone of faith will have a deeper affect.

So associate with those who have faith and absorb the faith from them, the person acquires faith by submission more than by learning. Look how they live, how faith appears in their lives, how they deal with God, and how they react towards certain circumstances. If you want to strengthen your faith then no doubt you need this quality.

5-Humility Of Heart And Mind.

The humble person accepts all what comes from God with satisfaction. But the mind that is proud of itself discusses, argues and refuses what doesn't please it. So it won't reach the faith the humble person reaches.

The humble person admits that his mind is limited and that his abilities are limited and that he cannot absorb God the unlimited, and does not perceive the depth of His wisdom and qualities. Thus he accepts in faith and does not doubt. If the mind presses down upon him, he would then lay down before God and say: "Your wishes O Lord are above my understanding and Your works are above my knowledge. Who am I in front of You? All my knowledge is ignorance in front of You".

I take from You via submission and not via inspection. Give me O Lord the faith of children and not that of philosophers and wise men (Luke 10:21).

Should we put the story of the three young men in the fire without being burnt (Dan. 3:25) in our limited understanding or should we accept it in faith, with a humble mind that bows down before the miracle? The miracle is the work of God who is able to do anything.

Faith needs the humility of the mind and the simplicity of the heart and it also needs:-

6-The Experience With God

Throw yourself in the circle of God, live with Him and test Him, try to rely on Him, at that time you will see His miracles working with you. If however you limit yourself, all your life, in the circle of the mind's abilities, the human wisdom, the experiences of society, the people's advice away from God, you eat everyday from the tree of knowledge... so how will you then reach faith? Therefore, test practically the existence of God in your life. Associate with Him so that you know who He is, and as David the prophet said "*Oh, taste and see that the Lord is good.*" (Ps 34:8). Maybe someone will ask: how can we experience God and I say:

7 - See God In Every Matter

People's faith does not grow stronger when they live in a world they separated from God. They give reasons to things that happen in this world without mentioning the name of God, as if the world rotates without God.

a- **An example**: man can destroy the atom, use nuclear energy, build space-crafts, reach the moon, rotate around the universe and deal with electronics... People then speak out: how great the human mind is! How great is the nation that invented all those things! They fait to mention God's name at all !

But the believer says: Glory be to You God the creator of this human mind. You granted him all the possibilities, and You revealed to him all the power You put in nature. If Your believers know all this, so how is it then with You? You who are unlimited, who can do anything? What strengthens the faith of the believer is that he relates every power and every miracle to God.

b- **Another example**: a person gets sick with a dangerous illness, and a doctor can save him from death and is healed. The sick person and his family admire the cleverness of the doctor, so they thank him in the newspapers and praise him, and consider him the cause for the healing. The name of God is never uttered on their lips.

But the believer says: we thank God that He healed the sick person, His hand was the doctor's hand.

c- **A third example**: a person is subjected to an accident that would have costed him his life, had there not been a driver who stopped the car a few centimetres apart from him. The people shout and say: how skilful the driver is, but the believer says: God granted this person a new life.

How beautiful it would be if you search for God's hand in every incident so as to strengthen your faith.

Search for God's judgement and work this in your daily life. At that time you will find God everyday, you touch and deal with Him, and you feel His presence in all what happens to you; small or big. In this way your faith will increase day by day.

d- **A fourth example**: if a believer passes by a garden and sees a flower it would not be suffice to enjoy it's shape and smell as the intellectual does, but will stand overwhelmed in front of it and will say: what is this beauty O Lord that you created? What are these wonderful colours that the most clever artists cannot create. No doubt the artificial flowers are accurate and beautiful but are not in this arrangement, besides that they are lifeless without ripeness or smell. It is dead beauty.

Really, contemplating about nature in this manner strengthens the faith.

People of the world admire nature as one; they separated it from God. However, he, who wants to strengthen his faith, sees God in nature. Isn't it His creation? This is how David the prophet says "*The heavens declare the glory of God; And the firmament shows His handiwork.*" (Ps 19:1). Do you admire a moony night without glorifying God the creator of the moon? Remember God in this way so that He becomes a practical reality to you and not just an intellectual reality to be proved with evidences ... in this way you will everyday live with God .

If you desire to strengthen your faith then don't separate God's creations from Him.

Do not be overwhelmed by the nature and forget God. Don't be overwhelmed by the human mind and it's dealing with the matter, but say: You are wonderful Lord! How did you create the material world like this with its qualities and effects so that the mind can use for all these aims. Do we wonder about a doctor who extracts a medicine from a certain material, whereas that we forget God who put this quality in this material so that it can serve the doctor's aim!

Another matter can strengthen your faith:

8-Take The Lord As Your Friend:

If you did this, it would strengthen your faith because you will build a relationship with God and talk with Him without fear.

Many look unto the Lord as God or master. But did you look unto Him as a loving friend, having confidence in Him and in His loyalty. He knocks at your door and asks you to open the door as a friend. He win enter and eat with you and you with Him (Rev. 3:20). If you accepted God's friendship and love, you will enter the real faith... you will look forward to seeing Him as a friend, to tell Him your secrets, and enjoy His companionship and love... you will take care as a friend not to hurt His feelings or make Him angry. He, Himself, will reveal His secrets to you as He did with Abraham (Gen. 18:17).

God wants you like this because He said "No longer do I call you servants… but I have called you friends." (John 15:15) so take Him then as a friend or Father, and believe in His sovereignty and power, and share your secrets with Him, and He will share His with you.

From the stories of friendship and truth with God is the anointment of Elijah to Elisha as a prophet.

One day the Lord told Elijah, the great prophet, "*anoint Jehu the son of Nimshi as king over Israel. And Elisha the son of Shaphat of Abel Meholah you shall anoint as prophet in your place.*" (1 Kin 19:16).

Elijah did not say well, Lord I will anoint Jehua a king, but how can I anoint a prophet in my place? Are you not in need of my services? Does this happen now after my great efforts for your sake, and after standing before King Ahab and his wife Jezebel, and after freeing the land from all the Baal prophets? Did Your love for me change?

Elijah did not say anything of the sort, and did not doubt in God's love, but did what God ordered, having confidence in God's love and wisdom. Elijah considered it familiarity and friendship with God. God made Elijah participate with Him in carrying out the Godly plan, even if he had to anoint a prophet in his place. This does not mean that the friendship between him and God is finished or reduced.

The proof is that God raised him, later on, in glory to Him in heaven (2 Kin 2:1 1). Further evidence that He appeared talking with him on mount Carmel. It is love that God made clear to him even in the matters concerning him. The anointment of a prophet in his place was the beginning of his promotion to a better state greater than being a prophet.

9-Prayer For The Sake Of Faith

Pray for your faith that it may grow and increase.

Tell Him: Give me O Lord, that I believe in You with full faith. Give me that I love and have confidence in You in everything, and to believe that You do me benevolences even if the world was dark in front of me. Let me feel that my mind is much smaller to understand Your wisdom and judgment. I know that You are a doer of benevolences, that You are loving, that You see everything and that You are capable of doing everything, and in spite of that my faith often weakens... so help my weak faith.

CHAPTER 9

WHAT WEAKENS THE FAITH

The devil labours continuously with all his efforts to weaken the believers' faith. He and his companions try to deceive even the elect (Matt. 24:24). It does not suffice them only to weaken the faith, but even to turn their victim into an apostate. This is how in the end of days many will abandon the faith "*Giving heed to deceiving spirits and doctrines of demons*" (1 Tim. 4: 1). How dangerous is the Bible's saying about the Second Coming of Christ "*Nevertheless, when the Son of Man comes, will He really find faith on the earth*" (Luke 18:8).

What are the demon's tricks to weaken the faith? There are many: some are terrible, and some are calm that nobody can feel.

1- The Self

The self often opposes and refuses God because He is against its sinful desires.

The self feels that God limits its freedom. It desires things God does not agree upon, to enjoy this (liberty) or this negligence, it thus separates itself from God, as the lost son did. He left his father's house (Luke 15:11-14), to spend his share of the money as he wishes ... or to refuse God. The apostates are examples of those who refuse God and their motto becomes:

It is good that God does not exist, so that I can exist.

These people have misunderstood the real meaning of existence and the real meaning of freedom. Liberty is not doing what one wishes, ones wishes may be wrong, but the true liberty is to be freed from all what assails the self... to be freed from bad habits that enslave him, and from the sinful desires that defiles him, and to be freed from the domination of material things on him. All that prevents the self from souring towards God and from being in God's companionship; which is the real existence.

From the hindrances of the self towards faith is the desire of man to feel himself, in power, greatness and pride and here God sees a rival.

Herod the king found that the new born in Bethlehem will share with him the reign, thus he refused to have faith in Him and tried to get rid of Him by killing Him. The Pharisees are also examples like Herod, who saw Jesus taking their place and familiarity as a teacher. They said one to another "*You see that you are accomplishing nothing. Look, the world has gone after Him!*" (John 12:19). Many refused the faith in Jesus Christ's resurrection because of their self, so as it won't be evidence against them being guilty of this man's blood (Acts 5:28) ... The self is the greatest hindrance towards faith. Accordingly, the Lord said: "*If anyone desires to come after Me, let him deny himself...* " (Matt. 16:24).

He also said "*He who finds his life will lose it, and he who loses his life for My sake will find it.*" (Matt. 10:39). Thus, Saint Peter the apostle says relating to faith "*... Nor do I count my life dear to myself, so that I may finish my race* " (Acts 20:24), "*I also count all things loss for the excellence of the knowledge of Christ Jesus my Lord, for whom I have suffered the loss of all things, and count them as rubbish, that I may gain Christ and be found in Him.*" (Phil. 3:8-9). Are you like that? or...

Is your faith hindered due to your self? due to your wishes, desires, ideas and passions?

Is there opposition between God and your self? If it so then deny your self, resist it, overcome it, because better is a man who controls his soul than one who controls a city (Prov. 16:32).

The Pharisees, scribes, and priests took much care of their selves. In each self, there were faults. Jesus used to discover these faults without having to speak about them, just by comparison it was revealed. For this reason they hated Him and didn't believe in Him because He was the light that endangered their darkness. Their selves were obstacles on their way of faith.

Not to forget that the devil's self was a reason for losing his faith.

When he thought of how to magnify his soul. How to ascend to Heaven and to sour up above the planets of God, and become like the Most High (Is 14:14), so the (greatness) of his self opposed his faith in God. As for the virtuous angels, they kept their places because, in their faith in God, they considered themselves "*His hosts, You ministers of His, who do His pleasure.*" (Ps 103:21).

Many find their selves beautiful in their eyes, their selves are their idols.

What prevents them from the life of faith: the self love, self esteem, the desire to magnify the self, to fulfil the self's passions, and to run away from everything that reveals this self and reveal it disadvantages ... thus they want their selves to live in an atmosphere of coquetry, courtesy and praise. They are annoyed from every sincere word, every reproach and every punishment. So how can they live in faith?

If you were like this, try to improve yourself so that you humble yourself before God and live in faith.

From the matters that also weaken the faith:

2-Domination Of The Senses.

This is what happened to Saint Thomas the apostle, when he refused to believe in the resurrection of the Lord and said "*Unless I see in His hands the print of the nails, and put my finger into the print of the nails, and put my hand into His side, I will not believe.*" (John 20:25). God condescended with the weakness of Thomas's faith and permitted him to become sure through his senses by saying "stop doubting and believe" and he rebuked him saying "*Because you have seen Me, you have believed. Blessed are those who have not seen and yet have believed*" (John 20:27,29). What the person sees we call observation and not faith, but it may lead to faith.

Is this faith weak? There is even worse: he who sees and still does not believe.

As an example of those are the priests who saw the empty tomb and did not believe in the resurrection. The Pharisees who saw the miracles of Jesus, like the healing of the born blind, and the raising from the dead, and did not even believe. Those refused faith due to reasons in their hearts. What our father Abraham said to Lazarus applies to them "*Neither will they be persuaded though one rise from the dead.*" (Luke 16:31).

3-Submitting Faith To The Mind

The mind has limits which can not be overcome and that faith is at a higher level than that. But there are people who want their minds to perceive the unlimited, the miracles, and what is beyond their understanding or else, they refuse all this!

They want theology to be submitted to scientific research and this is logically impossible. It is not reasonable that the mind, which is limited, subdues to the unlimited.

Maybe as an example of this, is what is known today as the 'New Theology', in some of the institutes, where they want to submit the soul and miracle to pure scientific research or to symbolic explanations. Thus they deny many of the miracles and many stories told in the Bible and mix it with Mythology! Really, the mind is lost if it tries to think highly of itself more than it ought to (Rom. 12:3), and thus it strays away from faith and tries to lead others in the same obliquity.

4- Associating With Doubtful People:

Just as associating with men of faith strengthens the faith, also associating with doubtful people plants doubt in minds and hearts. If it was persisting, or if, it has a deep effect or if the level submitting knowledge to doubts is lower than the mind, or if it was not deep enough in the faith.

For this reason the Bible prevents the association with apostates.

Saint John, the apostle, says "*If anyone comes to you and does not bring this doctrine, do not receive him into your house nor greet him; for he who greets him shares in his evil deeds..* " (2 John 1:10). That is why the church prevented the association with the heretics and the banished.

How many people associate with non Christian groups like the Jehovah witnesses for example, and the result is that they lose their directions. How many church members associated with strange groups or heretics and their beliefs where deeply affected.

Considering behaviour and spiritualities, the association with doubtful people weakens the faith:

You may be faced with a test or a problem and you accept it in faith, and you submit the matter to God thanking Him for everything. Then, a person with little faith visits you, and he keeps on explaining how dangerous the matter is and frightens you of its results, until you lose your peace of heart. It also weakens your faith in God's care and you get worried.

Be careful with whom you associate and with whom you mix your ideas.

This leads us to another point which also weakens the faith:

5- Yielding And Having A Weak Personality:

Mary Magdalene is as an example of those: she saw the empty tomb, heard the angel's good news, even saw the Lord Jesus after His resurrection, held on His feet, heard His voice, and He gave her a message... but after all that she said three times "*They have taken away the Lord out of the tomb, and we do not know where they have laid Him.*" (John 20:2,3,13, 1 5), and in this she denied the resurrection. What is the reason of this transfer? and how did her faith weaken after seeing Jesus and speaking with Him (Mark 16:9, Matt. 28:9)?

Mary Magdalene was young in age. Her personality weakened due to the rumours which the Jewish priests spread against the resurrection. She also weakened due to the disciples' non belief in the resurrection (Mark 16:11,13,14). Doubts and suspicions entered her heart, and she repeated it with her own mouth the rumours she had heard.

The faith of Mary Magdalene could not oppose the rumours and the people's talk.

She was inwardly moved due to the outer pressure and she yielded to it.

Many people are inwardly moved. They retreat. from their first faith, belief or behaviour, due to people's mockery and due to that their personality is being weaker than the opposition.

God wants your personalities to be strong. As the apostle says, "*Always be ready to give a defense to everyone who asks you a reason for the hope that is in you.*" (1 Peter 3: 1 5). The children of God are not weak. They should be like those whose faith or rather spiritualities are moved, and yield to any outer ideas, but apply what the apostle says "*Therefore, my beloved brethren, be steadfast, immovable...* " (1 Cor. 15:58).

Our mother Eve is also an example of the kind who deviated from faith due to yielding. She deviated from faith as she heard what the snake said and it resulted in her being sent out of Paradise.

How many go after rumours and believe them. How many utter words about the Second Coming and people believe them. They say the Anti Christ is born, is in an American State, and that he is now 17 years of age!! And also that the world will come to an end this year or another! How many dates did the Jehova's Witnesses fix about the second coming, and nothing has happened...

The faith of some may weaken and they would follow those who claim they saw visions and dreams.

They think that those who claim having visions and dreams are true and that they come from God! They are cheated by what he says, even if it was against their beliefs and spiritual principles. God warned against those people since the days of Moses the prophet, and said:

"*If there arises among you a prophet or a dreamer of dreams, and he gives you a sign or a wonder, and the sign or the wonder comes to pass, of which he spoke to you, saying, `Let us go after other gods'--which you have not known--`and let us serve them, you shall not listen to the words of that prophet or that dreamer of dreams, for the Lord your God is testing you to know whether you love the Lord your God with all your heart."* (Deut. 13:1-3).

Yielding is one of the reasons that weakens the faith. Another reasons is:

6-Fear

Fear weakens the faith and a weak faith leads to fear. Saint Peter, the great apostle, denied Jesus, when he feared. He insulted, cursed and swore that he didn't know the man (Matt 26:74), and thus his faith weakened. Jesus told him before that "*I have prayed for you, that your faith should not fail.*" (Luke 22:32).

Many lose their faith due to fear. That is why Revelation puts the cowards at the top of the list of perishers, and said "*But the cowardly, unbelieving, abominable... shall have their part in the lake which burns with fire and brimstone.*" (Rev. 21:8). The placement of the cowardly before the non-believers can mean that the cowardly, due to their fear, became non-believers.

Pontius Pilate believed, deep within, that Jesus of Nazareth was innocent of the charges set against Him by the Jews. He was confident that the Jews handed Him due to envy. He tried to set Him free and said about Him “this Holy person”... but finally he submitted to his weakness, and presented Jesus to be crucified because he was afraid the people would say about him that he was against Caesar...

As for the spiritual person, he doesn't lose his faith at all because he doesn't fear...

From the matters that also weaken the faith is:

7-Lust

Many lost their faith due to lust. As an example of those is **Demas** who was Paul's helper in preaching. Saint Paul wrote about him “*Demas has forsaken me, having loved this present world.*” (2 Tim. 4:10). Love of the world weakens the faith because it is hatred against God (James 4:4).

Also from the examples of those who lost their faith, due to lust, was **the rich young mn** ... He left Christ “*Sorrowful, for he had great possessions."* (Matt. 19:22). Thus, the lust for money may weaken the faith.

How many left Jesus for the sake of a woman or a position... **Solomon, the wisest on earth, lost his faith due to his lust for women .**

He "*Loved many foreign women* " (1 Kin 11: 1). "*When Solomon was old, that his wives turned his heart after other gods; and his heart was not loyal to the Lord his God, as was the heart of his father David. For Solomon went after Ashtoreth the goddess of the Sidonians, and after Milcom the abomination of the Ammonites. Solomon did evil in the sight of the Lord."* (1 Kin 11:4-6).

This great wise man fell, however we believe that he repented in his last days. The book of Ecclesiasts is evidence to his repentance.

Ananias and Sapphira lost their faith for lust of money, so they perished.

They both "*lied to God*" (Acts 5:4) and *also "tested the Spirit of the Lord*" (Acts 5:9). They both died perishing.

Balaam lost his faith due to his lust for money. He was a prophet and had beautiful prophecies about Jesus. Finally, he fell in darkness due to "*Wages of unrighteousness.*" (2 Pet. 2:15). He thus caused people to fall and taught Balak the way of sin (Rev. 2:14)... he and others perished.

The lust for greatness and overcoming others lead to the loss of faith of many:

Maybe one of those was Diotrephes who "*who loves to have the preeminence among them*". Thus, he opposed Saint John and drove away many brothers out of church (3 John 1:10)

The lust for Godliness lead the great Cherubim to lose his faith and became a devil. He was earlier an angel of light with greatness and beauty.

Indeed, lusts are from the matters that weaken and stop the faith. From the reasons that also weaken the faith are distresses and the pressure of outer circumstances.

8- External Circumstances

As an example of such cases is **Gideon.** When his faith weakened concerning the care of God, the angel told him "*The Lord is with you, you mighty man of valor!" Gideon said to Him, "O my lord, if the Lord is with us, why then has all this happened to us? And where are all His miracles which our fathers told us about, saying, `Did not the Lord bring us up from Egypt?' But now the Lord has forsaken us and delivered us into the hands of the Midianites"?* (Judges 6:12-13).

In this way, the faith may weaken if the distress lasted long or if it became stronger.

The faith of the disciples weakened and they doubted when the waves of the sea broke over the boat. They told the Lord "*Do You not care that we are perishing?*" (Mark 4:38-40).

When the Israelites stayed long in the service of Pharaoh they were discouraged and their faith in salvation weakened (Ex. 4:1).

There is another dangerous reason that weakens the faith:

9-The Devil's Deceptions.

Among these misleading are the false visions. Satan -so as to teach the people- "***transforms himself into an angel of light.***" (2 Cor. 11:14). He can even perform false miracles as it was said about the lawless one at the end of time "*According to the working of Satan, **with all power, signs, and lying wonders, and with all unrighteous deception** among those who perish.*" (2 Thes. 2:9, 10). The prophet said that this will cause the great rebellion before the coming of Christ (2 Thes. 2:3). Namely the loss of faith due to these Satanic misleading which deceive the people.

Satan may deceive people with dreams and false prophecies, with ideas, misleading and innovations so as to destroy the faith in their hearts... he may even send them "*false prophets will rise and show great signs and wonders* ." (Matt. 24:24). **He may tell them "here is the Christ".** The Lord warned "*If anyone says to you, 'Look, here is the Christ!' or 'There!' do not believe it.*" (Matt. 24:23).

All this needs setting apart, as the prophet said "*Do not believe every spirit, but test the spirits, whether they are of God;*

because many false prophets have gone out into the world." (1 John 4:1).

One of the main factors that weakens the faith is

10-Doubt:

Doubt weakens the faith and a weak faith produces doubt... This is exactly what we said about fear. Each of them causes the other or results from the other.

a- Doubt was one of the wars the devil fought against our first parents to lose their faith. He told them *"Has God indeed said ... you will surely not die?* " (Gen. 3:1-4).

   If you are faced with doubts concerning the existence of God or other principle beliefs then do not fear. These are from the enemy's wars and not your denial of faith, and especially, if your heart was refusing it. In such circumstances, you have to pray so that God lifts up these wars from you, and that you change your way of thinking, and occupy yourself with another subject. But if the doubts are from you and you are convinced with them so you have to treat them with a pure spiritual understanding by asking the specialists in theology, and by reading useful books in your subject.

   There are other wars against doubt lighter than this, we mention the following:

b- Doubt in God's aid or in that God has abandoned you.

The Lord rebukes this kind of doubt by saying "*O you of little faith, why did you doubt?*" (Matt. 14:31). Here He relates between doubt and little faith, because the person with a strong faith would never doubt in God's love and care.

They many perpetual distresses may sometimes press on the heart and one would say, "*Why do You stand afar off, O Lord? Why do You hide in times of trouble?*" (Ps 10:1).

This is blame and not weakness in the faith. It seems to the psalmist that the Lord is standing afar, but the Lord keeps guard with all love and care the security of His children, like the eagle that teaches its youngsters to fly, and like the father who teaches his son to swim. He leaves him for a while to train and gain experience. He watches him with all care. If He sees danger surrounding him, He will hurry to rescue him.

There is also the example of the mother who teaches her son to walk. She leaves him to fall down and stand up again to strengthen his bones and muscles and to learn. However, if she hurried to carry him in her arms after each cry, that will harm him, because he will not learn and his bones will not be strong enough.

The distresses are a school to train us to pray and to hold onto God. We are also trained in faith and we see how God

works, and with which strength. For sure, God works, in spite that we do not see Him and do not feel His work.

The person may doubt if he only looked to troubles and not to God. That is how we see Peter doubt when he looked to the water beneath his feet and did not see Jesus who held his hand. As the faith of Peter decreased so did he start to sink and then the Lord rescued him.

The children of God may be like “lambs among wolves” but they do not doubt or fear. As long as the good shepherd is among the lambs so the wolves and not even the lions will endanger them.

Our father Abram did not doubt in God's love and care, in spite of the difficulty of the matter of giving his son Isaac as a sacrifice, as if he were saying:

My heart is not tenderer than the heart of God on my son Isaac, and I can't manage the future of Isaac as God does.

As long as God agrees on something then, no doubt, I have also to agree upon it, because I do not have God's wisdom or love. So let it be His will.

He who does not doubt lives always in tranquillity and peace.

He always lives in security and the outer circumstances will not tire him. He does not impose on God certain solutions, and if God does not carry them out, he will be angry. Nevertheless, he agrees on any solution coming from God according to His Godly wisdom.

How many troubles does doubt cause in the heart and the mind... like doubt, fear, disturbance and little love. Doubt in itself is tiredness, a burning fire.

Doubt is heated by confidence and love. He who loves a person doesn't doubt in him. That is why we are with God and we do not doubt in Him because we love Him and have confidence in Him. Our faith in Him doesn't allow us to doubt in His Godly and Fatherly deeds with us.

Holy is He in all what He does.

Faith kids fear and doubt. Fear and doubt on the other side kill the faith.

Hold on to your faith because it is a strong and victorious element. You will then live in joy, peace, tranquillity, without fear, and without any doubt all the days of your life.

CHAPTER 10

THE TEST OF FAITH

Are You in the Faith?

There are many ways to test the faith. They could be all deduced from the preceding chapters. We want to say here that the apostle - in the life of faith - does not speak merely about faith, ie. to confine in the name of the Lord, but he specifically mentions:

1-Faith Expressing Itself Through Love (Gal. 5:6):

Test your faith in love according to what the apostle explained in (1 Cor. 13) "*Love suffers long and is kind; love does not envy; love does not parade itself, is not puffed up; does not behave rudely, does not seek its own, is not provoked, thinks no evil; does not rejoice in iniquity, but rejoices in the truth; bears all things, believes all things, hopes all things, endures all things.*" (1 Cor. 13:4-7).

Do you have all these qualities so as to have a sound faith? The apostle said "*And though I have all faith, so that I could remove mountains, but have not love, I am nothing.*" (1 Cor 13:2). With this love, you can examine your faith... Yet in general, you can examine your faith through your deeds.

2-To Examine Faith Through Deeds

This is because the apostle says "*I will show you my faith by my works.*" (James 2:18). Through deeds you can examine your faith if it is alive or dead because "*Faith without works is dead.*" (James 2:20), and a dead faith can not save anyone (James 2:14).

Saint Paul the apostle, spoke a great deal about the importance of faith. We see him say: "*They profess to know God, but in works they deny Him* " (Titus 1: 16). In his first letter to Timothy he stresses upon this point and says, "*But if anyone does not provide for his own, and especially for those of his household, he has denied the faith and is worse than an unbeliever*" (1 Tim. 5:8). The young widows overcame their dedication to Christ because "*they have cast off their first faith.*" (1 Tim. 5: 12). Those who love money "*have strayed from the faith* " (1 Tim. 6:10), and those who are interested in impure and false chatter "*strayed concerning the faith.*" (1 Tim. 6:21).

Therefore, the person's behaviour may be a test of his faith. Saint John the apostle, said "*I know Him, and does not keep His commandments, is a liar, and the truth is not in him.* " (1 John 2:4), "*He who says he abides in Him ought himself also to walk just as He walked.*" (1 John 2:6), and thus we say:

3-Examination Of Faith Through The Purity Of Heart

He who believes that God is in front of him, that God is holy and hates sin, that He is just and rewards everyone according to his deeds, fears to err in front of God, is ashamed to do any wrong, and is ashamed to hurt the heart of the loving God; if he does believe in God's love!.

Here the apostle **says "Whoever sins has neither seen Him nor known Him "** (1 John 3:6). For sure, he who sins doesn't have in mind that God sees, hears and records everything during his sin committing... and for sure he who does wrong doesn't completely believe that there is a God who "*Gives freedom to the prisoners.*" (Ps 146:7) hence, if one says to the oppressor "God is present" then he fears and trembles.

For sure, the arrogant or the inflated with pride does not feel at all that he is standing in front of God. When Herod spoke to the people they praised him saying "This is the voice of a God, and not of man". Herod was glad to hear this praise. He didn't have faith that God is in front of him, and for this reason, "*An angel of the Lord struck him, ... And he was eaten by worms and died.*".(Acts 12:21-23).

The real believer can be tested through religious devotion without envying the worldly matters. The believers are content with whatever the circumstances are (Phil. 4:1 1).

Another point in the life of faith is:

4-Faith Is Tested Through The Power It Grants That All Things Are Possible:

Do you have the power of faith that you feel that everything is possible?

As the Lord said "*All things are possible to him who believes*" (Mark 9:23). Do you feel that something is hard or impossible? or that your faith doesn't believe in God doing it? Do you doubt the matters that need miracles? Can you say what Saint Paul the Apostle said "*I can do all things through Christ who strengthens me.* " (Phil. 4:13). Are you moved by obstacles and difficulties that you say "its not possible". Does despair fight you?

Despair is against faith and against hope in all directions.

No doubt those who commit suicide have lost their faith and their hope. They felt that there is no solution. They also lost faith in life after death in eternity and their destiny in it.

Also those, who submitted themselves to the present situation, to external pressures or to sin, didn't have any, faith at all that there is power that can support and deliver them.

Faith is a power for those who can use it in confidence and without any doubt.

I fear that faith in the hand of some is used like the staff of Elisha in Gehazi's hand (2 Kin 4:3 1). I also fear the same thing concerning people who carry the cross on their hands: they care to carry it and to perform its sign without having faith in it. They carry the cross but do not have the power that is concealed in it and in its deeds...

Do you think that Moses's stick separated the Red sea? Or is it the faith of Moses carrying and using it in the name of the Lord?

Do you have the power of faith that Moses had when he stretched his hand over the Red Sea?

You often pray, but does your prayer have faith that it gives it strength? How wonderful is the Bible's saying about Elijah "he prayed earnestly" (James 5: 17). This prayer was not ordinary as the prayers of rest of the people, because it could stop the heavens from giving rain and another time it did.

Test your faith through the power you have as a result of your relationship with God.

5-Test Of Faith During Distresses.

Trials face every man. There is a big difference between the believer and the non-believer's souls that accepts this trial. **If the trial disturbs your peace then know that your faith is weak.**

The believer accepts trials believing that they are for the good and that God will solve them. He is not disturbed or troubled and his heart is not burdened with sadness and pain.

He faces it with three verses, "*All things work together for good to those who love God.*" (Rom 8:28), "*Count it all joy when you fall into various trials* " (James 2: 1), and also "*All things are possible to him who believes.*" (Mark 9:23). With this faith, his heart rejoices in the trial and people are comforted through his happiness.

The believer places God between him and the trial; the trial disappears and God appears. He remembers God's hand with the saints in all their trial "*The Angel of His Presence saved them.*" (Is 63:9). He remembers what happened to Moses, Joseph, David, Job, Daniel and the three young men. All these increase his faith in God and increase his confidence in God's interference and in His word. Thus he is not shaken in trial, he doesn't doubt, doesn't feel sad and doesn't feel anxious... but says with the psalmist "*Our soul has escaped as a bird from the snare of the fowlers; The snare is broken, and we have escaped....Our help is in the name of the Lord, Who made heaven and earth.*" (Ps 124).

He tells the Lord: as long as You accept the trial then I am happy with it.

I do not only accept it or approve of it, but I am happy that the Lord gave me the blessing of this trial... It is lovely what was said about the apostles after being whipped "*So they departed from the presence of the council, rejoicing that they were counted worthy to suffer shame for His name.*" (Acts 5:41).

The believer sees the door of God open in spite that all other doors seem to be closed.

He believes in God who has the keys of Heaven and earth "*He who opens and no one shuts.*" (Rev. 3:7). The believer chants with Saint John saying "*After these things I looked, and behold, a door standing open in heaven.*" (Rev. 4: 1). To test the faith is to see all doors open in front of you, and every time you see a closed door in front of you, you say: This is not the door God wants me to go through. God has many other doors open.

There are doors that are now closed but God will open them later on with this faith you can calm down.

6-To Test The Faith According To Some Commandments:

a- **From the means to test the faith: the tithes and giving's in general**, and especially if this believer was in need, or if he was asked to give from his belongings. The meek in faith say, "if the whole salary or the whole income doesn't suffice, then how is it if reduced by a tenth?" The believer says if I give my tithe, this will bless the rest will be suffice and will even increase.

The tithe is a spiritual test the Lord gave in Malchi: "*Bring all the tithes into the storehouse, That there may be food in My house, And try Me now in this, Says the Lord of hosts, If I will not open for you the windows of heaven And pour out for you such blessing That there will not be room enough to receive it.* ' (Mal. 3: 10). If the person - in spite of this Godly promise - doesn't pay, so no doubt his faith is weak concerning God's promise and blessing, and even previously the doubt in His commandment.

If this was His the feelings about tithes then what about His commandment : give to the one who asks you (Matt. 5:42), and what about the commandment "*Go, sell what you have and give to the poor.*" (Matt. 19:21), and what about "*Sell what you have and give alms.*" (Luke 12:33)?

In this way, your faith is tested: Is God capable of supporting you after you pay your share to the poor? Is He capable to support you without storing up treasures on earth (Matt. 6:19)?

b- Among The Commandments To Test The Faith: Keep The Lord's Day:

Do you rejoice in the Lord's day so that you can spend it with Him? Or do you prefer other several occupations than the Lord? Are material matters more important in your eyes? It's a test for your faith.

c- Also From The Important Tests: To What Extent Do You Love Prayer:

Do you forget it and some times time passes where you don't pray? Does it happen that when you stand up for prayer that you think how it will finish so as to occupy yourself with more interesting matters? Does it happen during prayer that you meander away in your thoughts and forget that you are standing in front of god talking to Him? If you are like that then your faith is not at all strong in God, in His companionship and in the pleasure of speaking with Him.

Thus if we put the remaining praying matters and the remaining clauses of the spiritual works, there will be a field for testing your faith.

7- Test Your Faith In The Extent Of Caring About Your Eternity:

Do you concentrate your mind and heart upon this world and how successful you are and how you enjoy yourself in it?

Are you interested in your eternity and your destiny in the other world, and how you prepare yourself for it, as the Lord says "*Let your waist be girded and your lamps burning; and you yourselves be like men who wait for their master, when he will return from the wedding, that when he comes and knocks they may open to him immediately. Blessed are those servants whom the master, when he comes, will find watching*" (Luke 12:35-37).

The spiritual wakefulness is a deep test of faith.

Where is the faith of those who neglect their eternity, where is their faith? Where is their faith in the other life, and their preparation for it with repentance and good deeds, with love and companionship with God, and with oil in their lamps?

8-Test Your Faith In The Correctness Of Belief

Is it a sound faith without contrivances, false beliefs, and particular understandings? Is it the faith that was once entrusted to the saints (Jude 3) and was entrusted to reliable men who were also qualified to teach others (2 Tim. 2:12). Is it in accordance with the teachings of the Bible, or do you follow people spreading their own teachings? With this, you can test your faith .I say this because belief has a practical effect on the spiritual life.

9-Test Your Faith With The Sound Qualities It Has

Is your faith a practical one? Is it firm that no outer circumstances can shake it? Does it weaken or does it have doubt? Is it filled with peace and doesn't fear? Do you know the life of submission and the obedience of faith? Is your faith a living and prosperous one? Does it grow and increase?

I don't want to mention the rest of the qualities of faith so that you can test yourself.

But if you want more measures, you can read this book again from the beginning.

Lightning Source UK Ltd.
Milton Keynes UK
UKHW03f1428190318
319681UK00001B/8/P

9 780994 542502